Paradise Lost and the classical epic

Paradise Lost and the classical epic

Francis C. Blessington

Routledge & Kegan Paul
Boston, London and Henley

First published in 1979
by Routledge & Kegan Paul Ltd

39 Store Street,
London WC1E 7DD,
Broadway House,
Newtown Road,
Henley-on-Thames,
Oxon RG9 1EN and
9 Park Street,
Boston, Mass. 02108, USA

Phototypeset in Great Britain
in V.I.P. Palatino by
Western Printing Services Ltd, Bristol
and printed in the United States of America by
Vail-Ballou Press

British Library Cataloguing in Publication Data

Blessington, Francis C
'Paradise Lost' and the classical epic.
1. Milton, John. Paradise lost – Sources
2. Homer. Iliad 3. Homer. Odyssey
4. Virgil. Aeneid 5. Homer – Influence – Milton
6. Virgil – Influence – Milton
I. Title
821'.4 PR3562 78–41305

ISBN 0 7100 0160 6

For Ann

Contents

Acknowledgments

The debts incurred during this study are incalculable, but I wish to thank in particular Professors Raymond E. Blois of Northeastern University and Barbara K. Lewalski of Brown University for much of my understanding of Milton. Professor Lewalski was patient enough to teach me some more by reading the manuscript in an earlier version, as was Professor Michael C. J. Putnam, also of Brown University, who glanced once more at a former student's Greek and Latin translations. My wife, Professor Ann M. Taylor of Salem State College, read through many drafts and made many valuable suggestions for which the dedication is hardly payment.

I am indebted also to the staffs of the Harvard Library and Bodleian Library, Oxford, for their cooperation and to Northeastern University for giving me sabbatical leave in order to complete this study.

To the editor of the *Milton Quarterly*, thanks are due for allowing me to use two essays of mine that appeared in that journal: 'Maia's Son and Raphael Once More,' VIII (1974), 108–13 and 'Abdiel and Epic Poetry,' X (1976), also 108–13.

I wish also to thank Mrs Pamela Robinson for her careful preparation of the manuscript.

Introduction

That Milton used classical models for *Paradise Lost* may be the stalest news in Milton criticism, yet the complex relationship between the poet and his classical parallels has not been fully probed. This relationship is especially significant when we consider *Paradise Lost* and its classical predecessors, the *Iliad*, the *Odyssey*, and the *Aeneid*. Milton so constantly invokes these epics as a background for his own that the dynamics of the relationship should form part of our appreciation of the poem.

In order to investigate this relationship, I have restricted my analysis to the classical texts alone, although there can be little doubt that Milton used many of the commentaries upon Homer and Virgil, but, since the evidence is not certain in telling us exactly what use Milton made of them and since the poet himself does not send the readers of his prose or verse in any certain direction,[1] I have concentrated on the parallels that Milton deliberately invokes. *Paradise Lost* is Milton's own commentary on these classical texts.

So far no extended work on *Paradise Lost* and the three major classical epics has appeared, although valuable analyses crop up in such wide-ranging studies as John M. Steadman's important assessment of Milton's debt to Renaissance theory in his *Milton and the Renaissance Hero* and in his *Epic and Tragic Structure in 'Paradise Lost.'* Charles Grosvenor Osgood analyzed Milton's use of classical mythology in general in *The Classical Mythology of Milton's English Poems*, while Friedrich Buff's *Miltons Verhältnisse zur Aeneide, Ilias, und Odyssee* intentionally listed rather than analyzed parallels between the four epics. Some of the classical background was analyzed by Davis P. Harding in his useful book, *The Club of Hercules: Studies in the Classical Background of 'Paradise Lost,'* although he ranges beyond just the three major classical epics and does not consider the entire poem. Many shorter studies are also of extreme importance because they have done much piecemeal to aid our understanding of Milton's use of the classical epic, especially the work of Douglas Bush, C. M.

Bowra, C. S. Lewis, and E. M. W. Tillyard.[2] Therefore, there is little reason to review here the concept of classical imitation in the Renaissance or Milton's use of the classics in general. For both these topics the reader is referred to the bibliography, especially the work done on classical imitation by McKeon, Seznec, Weinberg, and White. For Milton's attitudes towards the classics, the reader is again referred to Bush and Tillyard, and, for Milton's theory of the epic, to Steadman.

Many of these studies have looked primarily at Satan and have seen in him the classical tradition that Milton rejected in *Paradise Lost*. As a result, they have polarized, often by default, good and evil into Christian and pagan elements respectively.[3] This tendency has three unfortunate results. First, it implies that Milton found the classical epic tradition evil, something to be replaced by the Christian epic. Yet Milton did not replace the classical epic *in toto* but revaluated it by correcting Homer and Virgil wherever necessary and by extending them wherever he found them acceptable to reason and faith.[4] Second, this tendency oversimplifies Satan's role: he does not, in general, embody the classical tradition or the old heroism but represents a perversion of the values found in Homer and Virgil. Third, it neglects much of the epic background: it has not been sufficiently noticed that other aspects of the poem have a relevant classical background: characters such as the Father, the Son, Adam, and Eve, as well as the structure and the narrator. What I wish to show is that the relationship between *Paradise Lost* and the classical epic is more subtle and pervasive than has yet been recognized and that every aspect of the poem interacts with the classical tradition.

Far from rejecting the classical epic, Milton used it in two ways. He extracted from it some insights into the nature of man and God, philosophical and theological truths gleaned from Homer and Virgil, and he considered these poets as models worthy of imitation throughout even the most Christian parts of *Paradise Lost*. Every aspect of the poem gains force by being set beside the Homeric-Virgilian tradition. The *Iliad*, the *Odyssey*, and the *Aeneid* appear in many ways behind Milton's epic – comparison, contrast, imitation, illustration of pagan insight and pagan error, and extension in history, literary tradition, and epic dignity – but they are, as a unit, the most important literary context for *Paradise Lost* outside of the Bible.

My major concern is threefold. First I wish to show that the classical epic is relevant to all parts of *Paradise Lost*, so I have divided the book roughly into the three spheres of action – hell, heaven, and earth – and I have treated in a separate chapter the structure, style, and narrator. Second, I wish to explore Milton's various methods for invoking classical parallels: how he varied from direct allusion to subtle suggestion and from the reworking of a specific scene from an earlier epic (*retractatio*) to the conflation of several such scenes (*contaminatio*). The various methods should be evident from the analyses presented in the text. Third, I wish to examine how this synthesis of pagan and Christian elements relates to the meaning of *Paradise Lost*. Throughout this study, I have tried to provide new classical readings of the text or to develop known ones further.

In Chapter 1, Satan is examined as the antithesis of the true classical hero, true by the standards of Homer and Virgil, as well as of Milton. Satan is the embodiment of a corrupt classicism and parodies, in turn, Aeneas, Achilles, and Odysseus. His classical background falls into three distinct phases.

In Chapter 2, I have analyzed the classical background of heaven: the loyal angels, the Son, and the Father. These characters represent a synthesis of classical and pagan elements acceptable to Milton, a corrected, purified, and elevated version of the theology of Homer and Virgil and the antithesis of the corrupt classicism of Satan.

In Chapter 3, I have looked at the classical background of Adam and Eve who experience the conflict of these two forms of classicism. Their development is traced, in reference to Homer and Virgil, from the innocence of the pre-epic world, through the epic tragedy, to a new synthesis of Christian and pagan values.

In Chapter 4, I have looked at the poem broadly, examining its structure, style, and narrator as a development and a fulfillment of the classical epic tradition, a synthesis of the pagan and Christian epic.

Milton built his epic out of those of Homer and Virgil, like a cathedral erected out of the ruins of pagan temples whose remains can still be seen. In an age that pays little attention to the classics, it is all the more necessary to examine these remains which the architect deliberately left showing.

By this approach I do not mean to exclude others. Milton's eclectic mind sends us in many directions, and his cathedral has many parts. In this sense there should be no conflict between classical and biblical sources: they are bound to overlap, since Milton was determined to use common ground throughout the poem.

1 'Pellax Ulixes': the revaluation of the epic villain

Paradise Lost is perhaps the shortest route from the literature of England to that of Greece and Rome. It brings the reader into immediate contact with the *Iliad*, the *Odyssey*, and the *Aeneid* while it reassesses them and lets the reader feel the energy that is constantly released by the interaction of classical source and Miltonic imitation. No other work, except the Bible, is as relevant to *Paradise Lost* or as persistently evoked. Since Milton intended his poem to be read as a gloss upon these predecessors, it was necessary for him to link the opening of his epic solidly to its poetic ancestry. For this purpose, he begins with Satan in full classical panoply, wearing the armor of Achilles, Odysseus, and Aeneas.

Here we shall first glance at Milton's use of classical details that invoke all three epics; then we shall examine closely three phases of Satan's classicism. What is most important is not what classical patterns Milton created but how they give his own poem meaning. He did not invoke the classical epic in order to displace it, as has often been maintained, but in order to show that Satan fails to be an epic hero even by the criteria of Homer and Virgil. In short, Satan is a parody of Achilles, Odysseus, and Aeneas.

The way in which Milton parallels all three major classical epics at once is evident in the council in hell. First it resembles the rigged council in the *Iliad* (II, 53–394) where Agamemnon tricks his followers into thinking that they are debating a return to Greece, though he secretly steers the argument into an attack on Troy through the machinations of Odysseus and the other Greek chiefs who bring the rank and file into line. Satan likewise tricks his followers into believing that they are having a free discussion, in this case, that they are considering any and all plans for the future of the struggle against heaven, but secretly steers the argument into revenge through the machinations of Beelzebub who sways the crowd. When Moloch, Belial, and Mammon suggest alternatives, Beelzebub offers Satan's plan and quickly calls for a vote; when Thersites, like Belial and Mammon, argues against resumption of the war, he is struck down by Odysseus. The malcontents out of the way, both leaders do as they wish.

The debate reaches out to parallel the broader situation of the *Iliad*. The point of the debate is really whether to use force or guile for revenge against God. Moloch's suicidal proposal for a frontal attack upon the citadel of heaven and Satan's later wheedling plan of revenge seem to parody the straightforward tactics of revenge that Achilles uses in the *Iliad* and the subtle machinations of Odysseus in both Homeric poems. The debate in *Paradise Lost* centers upon which of these two, now perverted, classical modes of heroism will be adopted. If guile finally wins out, leading us to see Satan in the role of another Odysseus with a different kind of wooden horse, the motive of revenge brings him into the role of another Achilles avenging himself on another Agamemnon. The parallels between the destruction of Eden and the destruction of Troy are only suggested in these opening scenes; they become more fully developed later. The immediate result of the debate is that Satan sets off on an Odyssean journey which takes him by a monster who claims to be his daughter and who clearly resembles Circe. Thus he follows narrow passages of greater danger than 'when *Ulysses* on the Larboard shunn'd/ *Charybdis*, and by th' other whirlpool steer'd' (II, 1019–20).[1] If the Mediterranean has been displaced by the sea of Chaos, the underworld of the *Aeneid* has been displaced by the hell of Christianity. This parallel I shall develop in detail for another purpose later, but it should be noticed that the pattern of floating on a sea after a defeat, the discussion, the reconnoitring, and the adaptation to a new home for exiles is the same opening pattern in the *Aeneid* and in *Paradise Lost*. In fact, Moloch strengthens this parallel by alluding to the *Aeneid*, as B. A. Wright notes, by saying, 'Th' ascent is easy then' (II, 81) which parodies Virgil's 'facilis descensus Auerno' (VI, 126: 'easy is the descent to hell').[2]

Milton has so immersed himself in the three major epics that one detail could strike more than one epic at the same time. When Satan and his followers writhe on the Burning Lake 'Nine times the space that measures Day and Night' (I, 50) – just as they fell nine days from heaven (VI, 871) – editors usually note Hesiod's fall of the Titans which takes nine days also (*Theogony*, 664–735). We should also note, however, that the *Iliad* opens with a plague of nine days and that Odysseus, when he founders at sea, seems destined to experience the same nine days (e.g., *Od*. IX, 82; XII, 447).

More important than the parallels themselves is the effect the invoked passage has upon Milton's scene. After we are told that Satan has spent nine days on the Burning Lake, his first words, addressed to Beelzebub, echo the *Aeneid*: 'if thou beest hee; But O how fall'n! how chang'd/ From him, who in the happy Realms of Light' (I, 84–5). As Newton long ago footnoted, the parallel is to Virgil's poem, where Aeneas has a vision of Hector returning from the dead, 'ei mihi, qualis erat, quantum mutatus ab illo' (II, 274; 'alas, how changed from that which you were'). An allusion such as this is more than footnotes imply. The whole situation of Troy burning and Aeneas hastening into exile should be recalled. The parallel between the defeat of the Trojans and the defeat of Satan's forces shows how Milton has extended the conception of the epic from the earthly to the spiritual realm, how hopeless the plight of the rebel angels is, how pagan and un-Christian their behavior, and how ignoble their subsequent action when compared to Aeneas' and Hector's, heroes who served as models for Christian behavior during the Renaissance. By looking at Hector, Aeneas has a vision of death and must learn to accept defeat at the hands of the Trojans. The same vision appears to Satan but it is now the look of spiritual, not physical, death on the face of his companion; yet Satan, unlike Aeneas, does not heed the message. Parallels to the major classical epics ripple out like this one in such a significant manner that to follow them out is almost never an unprofitable exercise. The habit of classical editors of Homer and Virgil to put in the parallels that Milton made to passages like the above, a habit unfortunately dying out, and his influence upon translators show how strongly classicists can feel Milton's attempts at epic imitation and emulation and how Milton can be used to elucidate the classical poets.

If Satan cannot compete with his classical prototypes, he does adopt their philosophy – or at least he pretends to. When Satan first appears in the poem scarred by the lightning bolt, he looks more like the enemy of Zeus than the enemy of God, and the resulting pessimism revealed in hell is much like the futureless world of the classical epics. Like that world, the rebel angels believe, or choose to believe, that fate rules: Satan assures Beelzebub that 'by Fate the strength of Gods/ and this Empyreal substance cannot fail' (I, 116–17). This idea culminates in Belial's statement that 'fate inevitable/ Subdues us' (II, 197–8).[3] It is fate that controls the action in the three major epic poems: the fate that dooms Hector and Sarpedon, that returns Odysseus to

Ithaka, and that allows Aeneas to found Rome. Satan represents the Father as the crudest of classical godheads, one whom only 'Thunder hath made greater' (I, 258). This kind of broad allusion is common in *Paradise Lost* and places Satan in the epic tradition, so that we are forced to evaluate him in the light of these earlier epics.

For this purpose it will help to see the patterns of classical references that Milton has woven around Satan. The interaction between Satan and his classical parallels falls, despite the myriad allusions to all three epics, into three distinct phases, each phase formed out of one of the former epics. When Satan first appears in hell, his major frame of classical reference is the *Aeneid;* later when Raphael relates the war in heaven, the frame is the *Iliad;* and when Satan appears on earth, the frame is the *Odyssey*. Only by examining the dynamics of these relationships can we fully appreciate Milton's subtle use of the classical epic. In the first phase, Satan invokes Aeneas and his epic. For this purpose, Milton created his hell in the image of Virgil's. At one point, the fallen angels take to singing their own deeds in heroic song:

> Others more mild,
> Retreated in a silent valley, sing
> With notes Angelical to many a Harp
> Thir own Heroic deeds and hapless fall (II, 546–9).

This passage probably parodies Orpheus' appearance in the Virgilian underworld:

> nec non Threicius longa cum ueste sacerdos
> obloquitur numeris septem discrimina uocum,
> iamque eadem digitis, iam pectine pulsat eburno (VI, 645–7).
>
> (and the Thracian seer in a long robe plays an accompaniment with the seven different sounds, sometimes striking them with his fingers, sometimes with his ivory plectrum.)

But Orpheus is not singing his own heroic deeds; he is probably playing an accompaniment to the nearby dancers. The egotism of hell drives it to sing its own heroic song for it can think of little else. But it is not proper to see in this egotistical singing a condemnation of the classical epic in general, since the classical heroes did not sing their own deeds in epic form. The reference is to shorter heroic ballads that were sung by heroes, such as that sung by Achilles about his own sack of Thebe (*Il.* IX, 186–91).

Virgil's classical warriors do not, even in the underworld, sing about themselves.

Hell has other Virgilian roots, too. Milton's simile of the fallen angels lying in hell like fallen leaves has a particularly Virgilian color:

> His Legions, Angel Forms, who lay intrans't
> Thick as Autumnal Leaves that strow the Brooks
> In *Vallambrosa*, where th' *Etrurian* shades
> High overarch't imbow'r (I, 301–4).

Of the many sources for this simile, the most often cited is that of the unburied souls, whom Charon will not ferry across the river of the underworld: 'quam multa in siluis autumni frigore primo/ lapsa cadunt folia' (VI, 309–10; 'as many as the leaves that fall in the forest at autumn's first frost').[4] The Italian landscape, the context of the underworld, and the accursed souls of Satan's followers lead down to Avernus and enrich the texture of *Paradise Lost* by adding the Virgilian underworld. This parallel denigrates Satan by placing him at the bottom of the classical underworld – now one of the unburied pagans.

Milton's use of his epic sources sometimes has an effect upon the reader when he returns to Virgil. After reading Milton's parallels between the fallen angels and the revolt of the Titans against the Olympians and having seen Milton's heavy Virgilianism in this part of the poem, a return to Virgil reveals that the Roman poet had also plunged the offenders of Zeus into his underworld:

> 'tum Tartarus ipse
> bis patet in praeceps tantum tenditque sub umbras
> quantus ad aetherium caeli suspectus Olympum.
> hic genus antiquum Terrae, Titania pubes,
> fulmine deiecti fundo uoluuntur in imo.
> hic et Aloidas geminos immania uidi
> corpora, qui manibus magnum rescindere caelum
> adgressi superisque Iouem detrudere regnis' (VI, 577–84).

> ('Then Tartarus itself opens down and stretches beneath the shades, twice the distance one sees by looking up at the aetherial sky of Olympus. Here the ancient race of Earth, offspring of the Titans, hurled down by lightning, roll at the bottom of the pit. And here I saw the twin sons of Aloeus, monstrous forms, who undertook to break open great heaven with their hands and cast down Jove from his high power.')

These rebels may, now that we have read Milton, be interpreted as the fallen angels. Milton has already pointed out this Virgilian perception and has given us the archetypes to look for in the *Aeneid*. Lest there be any doubt about the parallel, and few commentators have overlooked it,[5] Milton locates his hell by the same compass as Virgil, if we subtract the emulation, Milton's distance being much greater than Virgil's:

> Such place Eternal Justice had prepar'd
> For those rebellious, here thir prison ordained
> In utter darkness, and thir portion set
> As far remov'd from God and light of Heav'n
> As from the Center thrice to th' utmost Pole (I, 70–4).

If Milton's hell borrows the architecture, the lighting, the songs, the simile of the leaves, and the punishment of those who attempted to overthrow the godhead, it can borrow even minuter details, such as the harsh grating of the gates of hell. Milton wrote:

> on a sudden op'n fly
> With impetuous recoil and jarring sound
> Th' infernal doors, and on thir hinges grate
> Harsh Thunder, that the lowest bottom shook
> Of *Erebus* (II, 879–83).

He deliberately recalls Virgil's:

> tum demum horrisono stridentes cardine sacrae
> panduntur portae (VI, 573–4).

> (Then at last the awful gates are opened, shrieking on their dreadful sounding hinge.)

The parallel has been noticed but not its ironic significance:[6] the passage in the *Aeneid* describes the emergence of the fury Tisiphone who is sent by Rhadamanthus in order to punish offenders who do not receive their punishment on earth. The invocation of this Virgilian premonition of divine justice and the ultimate control by the godhead of criminals and devils alike is appropriate for the beginning of Satan's journey to earth.

The openings of both poems, as I said earlier, are similar too. Just as in the opening of the *Aeneid*, Aeneas found himself driven upon the shores of Carthage by the wrath of Juno in the form of a storm and was forced to found a new home, Satan is driven on to the Burning Lake by the wrath of God, also in the form of a storm, and forced, like the other exiled hero, to found another home.

Both, we are reminded, will indirectly bring revenge upon their enemies by attacking those related to their conquerors. The exploration of the new lands, the councils, the building – Pandemonium and Carthage – and the resumption of the journey to a new land make the scenes similar in pattern as do the thunderbolts cracking about the heads of the two heroes.

But the two heroes, once they are paralleled, clash. We remember that Aeneas did not merit his punishment, that he was a victim of the fate of Troy and the wrath of Juno, but Satan is punished for his seduction of the rebel angels and the war in heaven. The world of *Paradise Lost*, we notice, has a different moral framework than that of the *Aeneid*; so for Satan to posture like the heroic but unfortunate Aeneas is ludicrous. The two heroes are placed side by side, and always Satan sinks in the balance. This contrast would be almost automatic during a time when Aeneas was proverbial for his virtue and piety. His behavior was a model even for Christians so that Satan, possessing a theology that Aeneas never dreamed of, looks the more degraded by the comparison.

Again and again Satan's resemblances to Aeneas are undercut. Both Satan and Aeneas mistake the place of exile for their new home. Both presume to substitute it for their lost land. But both are wrong, so wrong that both leave their new kingdoms in order to found another. But the motives contrast: Aeneas leaves Carthage because Jupiter commands it, while Satan invades the world in order to vent his revenge upon God and deliberately transgresses the limits of hell.

In order to widen the gap between Satan and Aeneas, Milton invokes a parallel between hell and Carthage. Both Milton and Virgil use the simile of bees in the first books of both poems (I, 768–75 and I, 430–6, respectively); these similes are used to show the architectural industriousness of Milton's fallen angels and Virgil's Carthaginians.[7] Not only does hell resemble Carthage, but Pandemonium resembles Dido's palace, as Newton pointed out, right down to book and line number in the two poems:

> from the arched roof
> Pendant by subtle Magic many a row
> Of Starry Lamps and blazing Cressets fed
> With *Naphtha* and *Asphaltus* yielded light
> As from a sky (I, 726–30).

> dependent lychni laquearibus aureis
> incensi et noctem flammis funalia uincunt (I, 726–7).

> (burning chandeliers hang from the gold ceiling and torches conquer the night with their flames.)

Milton's 'Cressets' translates the Latin of Virgil precisely, since these are the baskets of wax that hang from cords, 'funalia,' which Virgil meant, though he, through metonymy, used the cords for the baskets.

But rather than paralleling Satan and Aeneas at this point, Milton invokes a parallel between Satan and the victim of Roman heroism, Dido. The technique of shifting the classical allusion from hero to victim we shall meet again. Here, as we recall the Virgilian scene, our sympathies are, as usual, pulled in the opposite direction. Milton does not portray Satan and his followers sympathetically, the way that Virgil portrays Dido. Again the question of causation and moral responsibility makes the difference. The reader knows that Dido will be destroyed by Venus in order to protect Aeneas, just as later Carthage will be destroyed to protect Roman landed interests in northern Africa. Satan's building, on the other hand, is the product of pride and defiance of God. By remembering sympathy for Dido, the reader feels the contrast with the ignoble and un-tragic Satan.

But usually Satan parodies Aeneas throughout this phase. He has not really fallen into Virgil's hell as much as into a corrupt state of soul where he parodies Virgil's hero much more than he imitates him: Aeneas' capacity for leadership, friendship, obedience to god, love, concern for his offspring, courage, constructive action, and especially his piety are lost in Satan. Where Aeneas finds the truth of the future from Anchises in the underworld, Satan manufactures lies; where Aeneas leaves Carthage to found a kingdom, Satan leaves hell to destroy one. The two contrast almost at every point.

In the second phase of his classicism, Satan parodies Achilles and invokes the *Iliad*. This parody is more grotesque than the first. It begins in the opening of the poem, where Satan has decided upon revenge for slighted honor, as Achilles did at the opening of the *Iliad*, but does not become the primary classical parallel to Satan until the war in heaven.

The war in heaven has long been accepted as Milton's most Iliadic section of *Paradise Lost*.[8] The battlefield is sown thick with epic similes imitated from the *Iliad*. If the two Ajaxes move across the battlefield like the black cloud of a storm (IV, 275–9), Michael and Satan rush at each other as:

if Nature's concord broke,
Among the Constellations war were sprung,
Two Planets rushing from aspect malign
Of fiercest opposition in mid Sky,
Should combat, and thir jarring Spheres confound (VI, 311–15).

The Patristic identification of the fallen angels with the pagan gods lies suggestively behind the battle in heaven:[9] the fallen angels bleed nectar, like Aphrodite's anchor (V, 340), and are as easily healed (VI, 330–3). As Addison noted,[10] Moloch flees the battlefield bellowing after receiving a wound from Gabriel (VI, 361–2), just as Ares fled the battlefield bellowing, after receiving a wound from Diomedes (V, 859–61). Moloch's speech in the infernal council indeed made him, like Ares, the exponent of brainless warfare, as insatiable as Ares was reputed to be, until both are unmasked as cowards. A ludicrous parallel emerges when Moloch threatens to drag Gabriel by his chariot (VI, 357–9), as Achilles dragged Hector around the walls of Troy. With these parallels, Milton underscores the inglorious truths of Homer's accounts of battles when he relates the actions of the rebel angels. Milton could have used the many biblical accounts of war as the basis for his war in heaven, and archetypes would have emerged clearly enough, but he chose to be specifically classical. In addition to the above parallels, the whole presentation of the battle is in keeping with Homer and Virgil's imitation of Homer. We find verbal sparring preceding the encounters on the field as well as the use of the classical spear and shield in place of the usual Hebrew weapons, the bow and the missile.[11]

Satan's weapons specifically invoke Achilles: he carries the great spear and the great shield like his predecessor. His withdrawal from the world about him results, like Achilles', from 'injured merit' and he refuses, like Achilles, to pay homage to whom he claims is an equal. The Greek warrior maintained that Agamemnon took honor for himself, refused to reward those who helped him, and abused kings like himself who were the equal of Agamemnon (I, 149–71). Satan too rebels on the question of honor. He claims to have been improperly rewarded for his merit when the Son is elevated in heaven. He especially claims equality with God:

Our puissance is our own, our own right hand
Shall teach us highest deeds, by proof to try

> Who is our equal: then thou shalt behold
> Whether by supplication we intend
> Address, and to begirt th' Almighty Throne
> Beseeching or besieging (V, 864–9).

Just as Achilles withdraws and refuses to show *'αἰδώς'* to Agamemnon, Satan rebels and refuses to yield homage to God. Both refusals begin the action that leads to tragedy in both poems. The wrath of Achilles belongs to Satan, 'But his doom/ Reserv'd him to more wrath' (I, 53–4), the wrath that he first brings to hell and later to Eden.

But Satan's stance as an Achilles figure is undermined more than it is underscored.[12] The war is presented from Raphael's point of view, a point of view that we accept because angels tell the truth in *Paradise Lost* and because epic narrators tell the truth in epic poetry. Satan is the inversion of Achilles, a warrior who possesses the rhetoric but not the ability of a warrior. If Achilles could terrify his enemies by merely appearing on the battlefield and could conquer the greatest warrior of the opposing army, Satan never lands a successful blow and is felled by Abdiel, one of the obscurest of the loyal angels. Satan's military record, like his shield, is as 'spotty' as the moon (I, 291). If his shield is larger than Achilles', it does not contain the world like Achilles'. The world of *Paradise Lost*, to press Milton's parallel, could not, like Homer's, be represented upon a shield. Homer's world was the physical battlefield that existed in pre-classical Greece when civilization was continually swept over by invaders. Milton's battlefield is the soul, the spiritual battlefield; as Raphael tells Adam, he is only 'lik'ning spiritual to corporal forms' in telling the story of the war in heaven (V, 573), since his tale exceeds the limitations of human imagination.

In reverence, too, Achilles excells Satan. When Patroklos dies, Achilles does not eat or sleep till he avenges his friend.[13] In classical epic, those who oppose the gods are destroyed like Patroklos – only Diomedes succeeds when he wounds Aphrodite and Ares but he is helped by Athene (*Il.* V, 826–31). Achilles warned Patroklos against fighting with Apollo (*Il.* XVI, 93–4). Indeed, reverence for the gods is a virtue that Achilles is never without: in the midst of his rage for the lost Patroklos, he does not turn against the gods. Those heroes who do, like Mezentius in the *Aeneid*, Odysseus' crew in the *Odyssey*, or Satan in *Paradise Lost*, perish, for the world of epic poetry has always been theologically orthodox. Satan also contrasts with Achilles in his arrogant verbal treatment of his enemies on the battlefield. Both Satan and Achilles, when he is in his wrath, hurl insults at their enemies, although Achilles has the might to overwhelm his foes and Satan does not. Satan proves to be only a verbal Achilles. To hear his descriptions of the 'Glorious Enterprise' (I, 89) that Satan presents at the beginning of the poem, we should almost believe that indeed the throne of heaven was shaken if we did not know that it was the prince of lies giving military reports in order to remuster his troops.

The same kind of verbal distortions occur before as well as after the encounters on the battlefield. This kind of 'flyting' is common in the *Iliad* among lesser warriors than Achilles. The contrast between Satan's Achillean stance and his true place in the canon of great warriors is evident in this premature epic boasting – the mark of false or lost heroes who are the foils for Achilles. Here Satan sinks further in this contrast to his real stature as an epic hero. He is a false Achilles like many warriors in the *Iliad* – yet his martial ability does not reach even theirs. The premature epic boast signals a doomed warrior who is about to be punished for his rash claim, as when Tlepolemos brags to Sarpedon:[14]

> *'σοὶ δὲ κακὸς μὲν θυμός, ἀποφθινύθουσι δὲ λαοί.*
> *οὐδέ τί σε Τρώεσσιν ὀΐομαι ἄλκαρ ἔσεσθαι*
> *ελθόντ' ἐκ Λυκίης, οὐδ' εἰ μάλα καρτερός ἐσσι,*
> *ἀλλ' ὑπ ἐμοὶ δμηθέντα πύλας 'Αΐδαο περήσειν'* (V, 643–6).
>
> ('You have a coward's heart, and your people are dying. I do not think that you, coming from Lykia, will be any help at all to the Trojans, even though you are very strong, but subdued by me you shall pass through the gates of hell.')

Such boasting often signals the death of the boaster in the *Iliad*,[15] and Tlepolemos falls a moment later with Sarpedon's spear appropriately through his throat. Boasting on the battlefield is usually punished and reprimanded in the *Iliad*: when Meriones brags to Aeneas that the latter could not endure being struck by his spear, Patroklos cautions him about boasting and says the work of battle is in hands, not words (XVI, 626–31). The general attitude is summed up by Menelaos' words to Euphorbos: '*οὐ μὲν καλὸν ὑπέρβιον εὐχετάασθαι*' (XVII, 19; 'it is not proper to boast arrogantly').

But as Satan is both insolent and improper, he boasts prematurely to Abdiel:

Ill for thee, but in wisht hour
Of my revenge, first sought for thou return'st
From flight, seditious Angel, to receive
Thy merited reward, the first assay
Of this right hand provok'd (VI, 150–4).

Satan is rebuffed by Abdiel, who claims no self glory: 'His puissance, trusting in th' Almighty's aid,/ I mean to try' (VI, 119–20). Abdiel strikes and knocks Satan back ten steps. A similar encounter ensues with Michael, who draws celestial blood from his thrust at Satan (VI, 331–3), who had again resorted to boasting, though a little mellowed after the encounter with Abdiel. Like Abdiel, Michael ascribes his power to God: he tells Satan to flee to hell, 'Ere this avenging Sword begin thy doom,/ Or some more sudden vengeance wing'd from God' (VI, 278–9). The same 'flyting,' without the punishment, occurred in Eden, where Satan confronted Gabriel and the guardians of paradise with the same premature epic boast:

Then when I am thy captive talk of chains,
Proud limitary Cherub, but ere then
Far heavier load thyself expect to feel
From my prevailing arm, though Heaven's King
Ride on thy wings (IV, 970–4).

As the sequels show, 'Heaven's King' is now the force that prevails on the epic battlefield. This change turns the classical epic boast of the *Iliad* into blasphemy and the glory of battle into praise for God and not man. Man is not, in Christian epic, the measure of all things. In classical epic, power is the result of innate strength and speed, exemplified *par excellence* in Achilles. Classical heroes succeed or fail depending upon this gift of nature, unless the gods help or hinder them on the field. This help is rarely given, however, in spite of the frequent appearance of the gods in the battles in the *Iliad*; they do more coaching than killing. But in *Paradise Lost*, divine help is an absolute necessity. This change elevates the action of Milton's poem above the earlier epics in the sense that this encounter is a struggle against the godhead. It also diminishes Satan whenever we remember Achilles' behavior on the battlefield. Satan's struggles are on a higher but not wiser or more heroic plane that Achilles'. Satan's boasting again reminds us of those Homeric heroes who thought that they were Achilles and had to be cured of their 'hybris.' Homer too would disapprove of Satan's boasting.

Related to the epic boast is the sarcastic mockery of Satan and Belial, another aspect of the foils to Achilles. This mockery is the epic boast in reverse: it occurs after, rather than before, an action, but it reveals the same egotistic, un-Christian arrogation of valor to oneself. When Satan has discharged the cannon against the loyal angels, he exclaims:

> O Friends, why come not on these Victors proud?
> Erewhile they fierce were coming, and when wee,
> To entertain them fair with open Front
> And Breast, (what could we more?) propounded terms
> Of composition, straight they chang'd thir minds,
> Flew off, and into strange vagaries fell,
> As they would dance, yet for a dance they seem'd
> Somewhat extravagant and wild, perhaps
> For joy of offer'd peace; but I suppose
> If our proposals once again were heard
> We should compel them to a quick result (VI, 609–19).

The *locus classicus* for this mockery is Patroklos' mockery of Kebriones, whom he has killed with a stone. Here Patroklos, like Satan, is deluded by the success he has had impersonating Achilles. Again Satan's resemblance to a hero is to be turned into a resemblance to a related victim. Both impersonators are about to be defeated, but for a moment they are deluded with temporary success. Where Satan used the comparison to a dance, Patroklos uses that of a diver, in order to represent the tumbling charioteer:

> *'ὢ πόποι, ἦ μάλ' ἐλαφρὸς ἀνήρ, ὡς ῥεῖα κυβιστᾷ.*
> *εἰ δή που καὶ πόντῳ ἐν ἰχθυόεντι γένοιτο,*
> *πολλοὺς ἂν κορέσειεν ἀνὴρ ὅδε τήθεα διφῶν,*
> *νηὸς ἀποθρώσκων, εἰ καὶ δυσπέμφελος εἴη,*
> *ὡς νῦν ἐν πεδίῳ ἐξ ἵππων ῥεῖα κυβιστᾷ.*
> *ἦ ῥα καὶ ἐν Τρώεσσι κυβιστητῆρες ἔασιν'* (XVI, 745–50).
>
> ('Alas, how very light the man is, seeing how easily he tumbles. If he were somewhere on the fishy sea, this man could satisfy many men diving for oysters, leaping from a boat, even in stormy seas, seeing how easily he now tumbles from his chariot to the ground. Even in Troy, there are also tumblers.')

As Milton and Homer know, the false Achilles foolishly exults over his foes. Both Patroklos and Satan are defeated soon after their perverse mockery, and Satan's imposture of Achilles ends.

In dealing with the angels then, Satan is a parody of Achilles.

As a result his behavior does not destroy the old epic heroism any more than a mock epic would destroy a real one. It is Satan's purpose that is wrong. Those loyal angels who fight against him successfully are doing the work of the Father on the battlefield as is the Son later. The loyal angels and the Son are also, as we shall see in the next chapter, akin to Achilles, but their cause is right. Both Homer and Milton stress the impropriety and the futility of fighting against gods; Satan's behavior would be tolerated neither on the plains of Troy nor on the heights of Olympus.

While Satan is a perversion of Aeneas in hell and a perversion of Achilles in the war in heaven, he is a perversion of Odysseus on earth. Satan's resemblance to Odysseus has been noticed but not analyzed in detail; yet it forms the third distinct phase in his base classicism.[16]

This specific piece of epic counterpoint Milton had learned from Virgil. Virgil had taken Homer's Odysseus and had used him for the purposes of representing villainy, but he had taken him whole and had no second thoughts about the hero who had destroyed Troy. When Odysseus turns into Ulysses, he becomes cruel ('durus,' *Aen.* II, 762), the inventor of crimes ('scelerum inuentor,' II, 164), and deceitful ('pellax,' II, 90). Virgil supplies a new Odysseus, Aeneas, renowned for his piety, to replace the inventor of crimes. Aeneas travels the same route but is incapable of deceit. Milton's technique is subtler, but he had learned from Virgil, and, as usual, he went further. Like the other two classical parallels, this parallel begins in the underworld. Satan gradually steers the argument of the war council from force to guile. When Beelzebub proposes Satan's plan for reconnoitring in Eden, he calls immediately for a vote. Since the infernal mob has been swayed with every speaker, this move insures that Satan's plan will be the one adopted. From there, it is a matter of course that Satan will be the one to hazard the journey. Satan remains the master of schemes throughout *Paradise Lost*, just as Odysseus is the traditional master of schemes in epic poetry before him. Satan invents the cannon during the war in heaven and successfully undermines the happiness of Adam and Eve. Both triumphs result from guile. Odysseus' plans are equally guileful, destructive, and successful: he plots the death of the suitors on Ithaka as well as the destruction of Troy, the latter by the stratagem of the wooden horse. If Satan is more destructive than his epic predecessor, he is also more perverse. Unlike Satan, Odysseus was viewed both as a model of virtue and a model for vice during the

Renaissance, although his habit of ready lying, which he shares with Satan, has always cast some ambiguity upon him as a hero.[17]

As Steadman pointed out,[18] Satan shares Odysseus' rhetorical power as well as his guile. Both are expert in councils and attempt to use intelligence as the means to escape, a device that saves Odysseus from the Cyclops and Satan from the sharp eyes of Uriel. Both disguise themselves physically as well as verbally: Satan appears to Uriel as a cherub and Odysseus turns up at the court in Ithaka as a beggar. Unlike Odysseus', however, Satan's ruses do not always succeed: he is captured in Eden while in the shape of a toad by the guardians of paradise.

Moreover, there is a difference between the treachery of Odysseus and that of Satan. The *Odyssey* has a clear moral polarity: the monsters and the suitors are evil and Odysseus, his family, and some servants are good. His treachery is the result of the will to survive and he always acts, like Achilles, in accord with Olympus. His only real fault is an over-active curiosity, which leads to the loss of some of his crew, as in his visit to the land of the Laistrygonians. Satan's motives on the other hand are deep-seated failings of character: his wounded vanity and his desire for power.

These contrasts emerge from the carefully conceived allusions to Odysseus that follow Satan once he leaves hell. That his journey through the sea of Chaos is the equivalent of Odysseus' ocean voyage and that Satan is harder tried than 'when *Ulysses* on the larboard shunn'd/ *Charybdis*, and by th' other whirlpool steer'd' (II, 1019–20) have already been cited as specific allusions. To these parallels must be added the conflict between civilization and chaos which lies at the heart of both poems. The tempestuous sea and the slowly dissolving kingdom of Ithaka in the *Odyssey* are what Odysseus must conquer, the first by endurance and the second by schemes and violence. The action of the poem is the struggle between civilization and chaos: whether society will dissolve back into its primal confusion or whether order will be restored. In *Paradise Lost*, the same question arises: will Satan return Eden and its inhabitants back into chaos? Will he undo creation? The roles of the two heroes, of course, are conspicuously reversed: Satan is the destroyer, not the preserver of society.

Another allusion widens the Homeric backdrop: Satan meets a new Scylla, Sin, in the company of Death: 'Far less abhorr'd than these/ Vex'd *Scylla* bathing in the Sea that parts/ *Calabria* from the hoarse *Trinacrian* shore' (II, 659–61). Here Milton perhaps reminds us that Scylla was probably only a rock in what are now the Straits of Messina. This deflating of classical epic is carried further by equating her with Sin, thus allegorizing Homer. It is Sin that is real and more dangerous than the monster that Odysseus confronts. Milton's use of allegory is unusual, however, a practice in keeping with Homer and Virgil who only let Delusion and 'Fama' slip into their epics for a short time. All three poets prefer fable to allegory, full characters to abstractions.[19]

Satan's reaction to this encounter is also Odyssean. Death raises his dart to kill him but Sin blurts out that they are all three incestuously related. Satan does not remember for certain that Sin is his daughter, but he reacts with Odyssean ambiguity: 'the subtle Fiend his lore/ Soon learn'd, now milder and thus answer'd smooth,/ Dear Daughter, since thou claim'st me for thy Sire' (II, 815–17). Satan's lore is that of the wily epic hero, like Odysseus, '*ὁ πολύτροπος ἀνήρ*,' the 'man of many turns.'

As a symbol of Odysseus' polytropic nature, Homer introduced Proteus, who is difficult to capture because he shifts into different forms: '*πάντα δὲ γιγνόμενος πειρήσεται, ὅσσ' ἐπὶ γαῖαν/ἑρπετὰ γίγνονται καὶ ὕδωρ καὶ θεσπιδαὲς πῦρ*' (IV, 417–18; 'He will struggle, turning into all things, into as many as there are beasts upon the earth, into water, and into blazing fire'). When Menelaos seizes Proteus, he turns into a 'strong-bearded lion,' then a snake, then a leopard, then a great boar, then 'liquid water,' and finally 'a tree with lofty leaves.'

> *ἀλλ ἤ τοι πρώτιστα λέων γένετ' ἠϋγένειος,*
> *αὐτὰρ ἔπειτα δράκων καὶ πάρδαλις ἠδὲ μέγας σῦς·*
> *γίγνετο δ' ὑγρὸν ὕδωρ καὶ δένδρεον ὑψιπέτηλον* (IV, 456–8).

Proteus' transformations vaguely proceed towards the stable and manageable, as Menelaos' grip holds and the fight goes out of him. Satan also goes through a series of transformations, but his mobility increases as his form degenerates, from the cherub who deceived Uriel to the cormorant who sits in the tree of life, an emblem of the great scavenger of human life. Satan assumes a variety of shapes in order to listen to Adam and Eve in the garden. These shapes resemble Proteus' but are marred by the images of destruction rather than left as symbols of courage:

> Down he alights among the sportful Herd
> Of those fourfooted kinds, himself now one,
> Now other, as thir shape serv'd best his end

> Nearer to view his prey, and unespi'd
> To mark what of thir state he more might learn
> By word or action markt: about them round
> A Lion now he stalks with fiery glare,
> Then as a Tiger who by chance hath spi'd
> In some Purlieu two gentle Fawns at play,
> Straight couches close, then rising changes oft
> His couchant watch, as one who chose his ground
> Whence rushing he might surest seize them both
> Gript in each paw (IV, 396–408).

Satan later becomes the serpent of the fall, thus completing the degeneration of the cherub who deceived Uriel. Milton has taken care to exceed Homer's description of Proteus both in the number of transformations and in dèliberateness of purpose. He also passes moral judgment on this polytropic behavior: Satan is forced to repeat his transformation into a serpent yearly and eat ashes off a tree in hell. Satan falls below even Proteus, the parody of Odysseus, as he fell below the parodies and victims of Achilles and the victim of Aeneas, Dido.

The return to hell completes Satan's Odyssean phase. Milton has incorporated the epic of return ('nostos') into his poem as Virgil did into his. Satan, the epic voyager, returns home and presents his visit to Eden as a heroic undertaking:

> Long were to tell
> What I have done, what suffer'd, with what pain
> Voyag'd th' unreal, vast, unbounded deep
> Of horrible confusion (X, 469–72).

These could be the words of Odysseus at Alcinoos' court if Odysseus had been self-glorifying. Satan's boast is that he destroyed paradise 'with an apple' (X, 487), perhaps a reminder of the Apple of Discord that caused the Trojan War which ultimately destroyed the city. Satan has destroyed Eden by testing its inhabitants, just as Odysseus tested the suitors of Ithaka and then destroyed them. Both testers don disguises for the purpose and employ craft as the means of discovering weaknesses. But the comparison leads immediately to the contrast. The purposes of both 'heroes' are opposite. Odysseus tests for the loyalty of the suitors; Satan tests for the disloyalty of Adam and Eve. In spite of his failings, Odysseus was the exemplar of passive suffering and active intelligence, but Satan is the perversion of these ideals, an Odysseus whose only purpose is destruction. If Odysseus can trick his household, he cannot deceive Athene; if Satan deceives angels, a third of the multitude of heaven, he cannot deceive the Father. If Odysseus finds his son who represents future life, the continuance of the race, Satan finds his son too, but he is Death, the spirit of negation.

This parallel continues in the sequel to Satan's last visit to Eden. In punishment for his Odyssean seduction of Eve, Satan receives a punishment similar to that of Tantalus in the *Odyssey* (XI, 582–92): when he tried to eat the pomegranates and apples, they moved away from him, just as Satan is foiled when he bites the fruit of the tree in the underworld and the fruit dissolves into ashes. Like Tantalus, Satan is condemned to repeat his futile action endlessly. Similarly, the hissing that God forces upon the fallen angels (X, 508) also has a counterpart in the *Odyssey* when Athene forces uncontrollable laughter upon the suitors (XX, 345–9) as a signal of their coming defeat and a symbol of their loss of power over Ithaka. The prophecy of Zeus at the beginning of the *Odyssey* that Odysseus would regain his kingdom has come true and so has the Father's prophecy that Satan's punishment would 'redound' upon his own head. In the end, Satan is not the returning hero but the guilty victim. God triumphs in both poems on the side of righteousness. Homer and Milton meet once more on common ground.

Whether Satan is shadowing Odysseus, Achilles, or Aeneas, he represents perversions of the classical world that followed the fall of Eden.[20] Satan is made the archetype of the sophistical rhetoric, the shallow egotism, and the destructive pride, the vices of the classical epic as well as of the classical world. In addition, he is the perversion of classical heroic virtues. He often begins by resembling a hero but ends by resembling a victim, sometimes even a perversion of that: he slips from Aeneas to Dido, from Achilles to Patroklos, and from Odysseus to the suitors. But even when he most resembles his prototypes, he does not displace them. Satan's classicism is far away from that of Homer's and Virgil's. Those authors would agree with Milton that Satan is not a classical hero but a classical villain who unheroically defeats creatures far below him in stature. He would have no place in the Greek or Roman epics.

2 Above the Olympian Mount

The classical background of *Paradise Lost* is not confined to Satan but stands behind every aspect of the poem, even the loyal angels, the Son, and the Father – a point not treated by criticism, except in the case of Raphael. While the Bible prescribes the orthodox limits for the development of Milton's God and His followers, the classical epic provides them with the virtues of the classical hero and the true theological insights of Homer and Virgil. As a result, the inhabitants of heaven mingle with the inhabitants of the heroic world, and the two worlds thereby merge rather than conflict. If Milton had wanted to oppose Christian and pagan values, he could easily have done so: his God did not have to wield the thunderbolt. Once He does, however, He becomes Zeus through theocrasia and helps to fuse the two worlds. In many of the aspects of his heaven, Milton sought for common ground between biblical and classical parallels. The antithesis of Milton's heaven is not the classical epic but the degenerate classical values of Satan. In order to examine the classical background of Milton's heaven, we turn first to two of the most important angels and then to the Son and the Father.

We start with Abdiel, one of the obscurest angels in the poem. He belongs to a type of character that, for a lack of a better name, I shall call the 'epic malcontent.' He appears throughout the epic tradition, usually in only one scene, and is otherwise absent. His function is to oppose the hero, who is about to undertake a glorious, usually martial, adventure, as we noticed earlier in the behavior of Belial and Mammon. The hero usually announces his intention at a council whereupon the epic malcontent rises in opposition, is scorned both by the hero and the assembly, and ultimately fails to stop the impending adventure. Yet, his objections express a groundswell of feeling that only he is courageous enough to utter. This feeling is often shared by the poet himself who in the broad canvas of the epic can include alternatives to the heroic code. At first, only the second thoughts of the poet are expressed by the epic malcontent, but Milton changed the tradition so that the malcontent is the true hero who opposes the egotistic heroic code of Satan with the humility of Christianity. I do not mean that the development of this figure is deliberate; it is the natural movement of society away from the heroic to the more sophisticated and civilized. But Abdiel's classical epic ancestors help us to understand how Milton was using him. Though other analogues exist in epic poetry (Milton developed Abdiel through *contaminatio*), I shall concentrate on one episode from antiquity.[1]

As we have seen, for the war in heaven Milton drew heavily upon Homer: the council of war, the description of the fighting in which individual combat is prefaced by dialogue and sometimes vain boasting, the instruments of war, the emphasis upon the raucous din of battle, the similes, and the deliberate allusions make a series of consistent references that often recall the *Iliad*. The classically educated reader of the Renaissance would probably recall the second book of the *Iliad* as he read Raphael's account of the origins of the war in heaven. In Homer, Zeus sends a false dream to delude Agamemnon into thinking the time has come to capture Troy. The dream, assuming the guise of Nestor, addresses the king:

> *'εὕδεις, 'Ατρέος υἱὲ δαΐφρονος ἱπποδάμοιο· '*
>
> ('You are sleeping, fiery-hearted son of Atreus the tamer of horses') (II, 23).

In *Paradise Lost*, as Bush notes in his edition of Milton, Satan whispers to the sleeping Beelzebub: 'Sleep'st thou, Companion dear, what sleep can close/ Thy eye-lids?' (V, 673–4). Both Agamemnon and Beelzebub are urged to marshal their troops and to consult their subordinate officers before assembling the rest of the army. Both commanders are deluded into thinking that they can now conquer their enemies. At this point, Homer and Milton both foreshadow the failure of these undertakings and remind the reader that both ventures are contrary to the will of the godhead. The passages are sarcastic and diminish the heroism of each attempt. Homer speaks in his own voice:

> *νήπιος, οὐδὲ τὰ ᾔδη ἅ ῥα Ζεὺς μήδετο ἔργα·*
> *θήσειν γὰρ ἔτ' ἔμελλεν ἐπ' ἄλγεά τε στοναχάς τε*
> *Τρωσί τε καὶ Δαναοῖσι διὰ κρατερὰς ὑσμίνας* (II, 38–40).
>
> (Fool, he did not know what plans Zeus devised: he was still to cause pain and groaning to Trojans and Danaans alike in the hard battles.)

Milton lets the Father Himself scoff at the rebel angels by pretending that He fears the overthrow of Heaven (V, 719–32). To which mockery, the Son speaks in a tone similar to that of the pagan poet:

> Mighty Father, thou thy foes
> Justly hath in derision, and secure
> Laugh'st at thir vain designs and tumults vain (V, 735–7).

After both poets have placed their deluded militants in unsympathetic perspectives, the epic malcontent appears with his objections, not just to the immediate situation, but to the whole heroic code. In the *Iliad*, Thersites rises to oppose Agamemnon:

> *''Ἀτρεῖδη, τέο δὴ αὖτ' ἐπιμέμφεαι ἠδὲ χατίζεις;*
> *πλεῖαί τοι χαλκοῦ κλισίαι, πολλαὶ δὲ γυναῖκες*
> *εἰσὶν ἐνὶ κλισίῃς ἐξαίρετοι, ἅς τοι 'Ἀχαιοὶ*
> *πρωτίστῳ δίδομεν, εὖτ' ἂν πτολίεθρον ἕλωμεν.*
> *ἦ ἔτι καὶ χρυσοῦ ἐπιδεύεαι, ὅν κέ τις οἴσει*
> *Τρώων ἱπποδάμων ἐξ 'Ἰλίου υἷος ἄποινα,*
> *ὅν κεν ἐγὼ δήσας ἀγάγω ἢ ἄλλος 'Ἀχαιῶν,*
> *ἠὲ γυναῖκα νέην, ἵνα μίσγεαι ἐν φιλότητι,*
> *ἥν τ' αὐτὸς ἀπονόσφι κατίσχεαι; οὐ μὲν ἔοικεν*
> *ἀρχὸν ἐόντα κακῶν ἐπιβασκέμεν υἷας 'Ἀχαιῶν.*
> *ὦ πέπονες, κάκ' ἐλέγχε', 'Ἀχαιΐδες, οὐκέτ' 'Ἀχαιοί,*
> *οἴκαδέ περ σὺν νηυσὶ νεώμεθα, τόνδε δ' ἐῶμεν*
> *αὐτοῦ ἐνὶ Τροίῃ γέρα πέσσέμεν, ὄφρα ἴδηται*
> *ἤ ῥά τί οἱ χἠμεῖς προσαμύνομεν, ἦε καὶ οὐκί·*
> *ὅς καὶ νῦν 'Ἀχιλῆα, ἕο μέγ' ἀμείνονα φῶτα,*
> *ἠτίμησεν· ἑλὼν γὰρ ἔχει γέρας, αὐτὸς ἀπούρας.*
> *ἀλλὰ μάλ' οὐκ 'Ἀχιλῆϊ χόλος φρεσίν, ἀλλὰ μεθήμων·*
> *ἦ γὰρ ἄν, 'Ἀτρεῖδη, νῦν ὕστατα λωβήσαιο'* (II, 225–42).

> ('Son of Atreus, what do you find fault with or ask for now? Your tents are full of bronze and in your camp are many choice women, whom we Achaians give you first whenever we sack a city. Do you still want the gold which some one of the horse-taming Trojans will bring you as his son's ransom out of Ilium, one whom I or another of the Achaians has bound and led away? Or is it for a young woman with whom you may mingle in love and keep apart for yourself? It is not right for you, the commander, to lead the sons of the Achaians into disaster! O weaklings, cowardly disgraces, daughters not sons of the Achaians, let us go homeward with our ships and leave him here to enjoy his gift of honor in Troy so he may know whether or not we are helping him at all. Now he has dishonored Achilles, a far better man than he. Seizing his gift

> of honor, he keeps her, himself taking her away, but no wrath remains in Achilles' heart; he desists. If there were, Son of Atreus, you would be maltreating someone for the last time.')

Thersites is the only common soldier that Homer mentions by name in the *Iliad*, and he appears only in this scene. In addressing Agamemnon, he reduces the heroic venture of the Trojan war to greed, lust, and egotism. He is denounced by Odysseus who strikes him on the back with his sceptre, since nine years of warfare would be wasted if Thersites' sentiments became general. But, although Homer and his Ionian audience undoubtedly sympathized with the Greeks, Thersites' objections have weight; they are echoed many times in the poem by Greeks and Trojans.[2] Homer's treatment of him is slightly ambiguous. Though Thersites is ugly and scurrilous, the soldiers grieve for him beneath their laughter when he is struck by Odysseus, and his name, which means 'bold,' can have the sense of either 'brave' or 'quarrelsome.' Only he has the courage to express the disillusionment that many feel because of the length of the war, though this disillusionment is evident in the surreptitious sympathy which Thersites arouses in the assembly (l. 270) and in the other expressions of disgust with the war found in the poem. Thersites is silenced but not before he raises objections that stay in the mind of the reader during the rest of the poem and slightly temper his admiration for the heroics of battle. Thersites' speech shows that Homer is not an unquestioning admirer of the heroic code. Aside from Thersites, the other soldiers remain in hierarchical submission and promptly ignore any legitimate objections that Thersites raised to the heroic code of behavior. Force wins out, and the mob falls in line – there was nothing wrong with Homer's psychology.

The similarities to *Paradise Lost* seem evident. Like Thersites, Abdiel appears in order to denigrate Satan's 'heroic' behavior, the assertion of the will of the hero against what seems to him a disparagement of his honor. Just as Thersites reminds Agamemnon that Achilles is a far better warrior, so Abdiel reminds Satan that he is inferior to God and that his attempt to stand against Him is hybristic:

> Cease then this impious rage,
> And tempt not these; but hast'n to appease
> Th' incensed Father, and th' incensed Son,
> While Pardon may be found in time besought (V, 845–8).

He reminds Satan of the hierarchy of heaven as Thersites

reminds Agamemnon of the hierarchy of the Greek army. The Son created Satan and the angels and is therefore their natural superior. Agamemnon is not only inferior to Achilles on the battlefield; he has abused his position as chief of the Greek forces by treating Achilles more basely than their almost equal status allows. Just as Thersites is used to express a general feeling that pervades the whole assembly, so by the same epic convention, Abdiel's sentiments should be extended to some of his less courageous companions.

Once this Homeric parallel is recognized, however, the differences also have an effect upon the reader. The heroic temper of the Homeric epics has been partly represented in *Paradise Lost* by Satan, who often parodies the classical heroes. If in *Paradise Lost* the degenerate epic hero has been equated with Satan, the epic malcontent speaks for God. Thersites' objections can only be the momentary consideration of an impractical alternative; Achilles must return to the field or his memory will be inglorious. His reputation depends not only on the men he kills but also on the quality of these men, but, no matter how sensible the objections of Thersites and Achilles may seem to the modern reader, given the terms of the *Iliad*, Achilles' faults do not lie in fighting *per se*, but in the 'hybris' of his withdrawal and in the mercilessness of his return. In Milton's poem, the positions of hero and malcontent are reversed: Abdiel's arguments against pride and disobedience reflect the proper moral attitude of the malcontent opposed to egotism. Compared to Satan, the malcontent is the hero.

Just as Thersites' objections were echoed later in the *Iliad*, so Abdiel's attack on Satan's martial 'hybris' is echoed by Michael, who tells Adam of the heroic age to come: 'For in those days Might only shall be admir'd/ And Valor and Heroic Virtue call'd' (XI, 689–90). The epic voice too denounces misguided heroism: 'Wars, hitherto the only Argument/ Heroic deem'd, chief maistry to dissect/ With long and tedious havoc fabl'd Knights/ In Battles feign'd' (IX, 28–31). These comments are not the voices of disillusionment that arise from Homer's characters and that must be quickly suppressed in the world of epic heroism. When Abdiel succeeds in opposing the hero, the basis of the Homeric code is criticized but not rejected. The question asked by Abdiel and echoed by Michael and the narrator is essentially: what is the fighting for? It is not that might should not be admired at all, but its purpose and object must be examined. In Milton's poem,

Abdiel asks the same question as Thersites but with a theological turn: is it proper to fight against God? The answer, as always in epic poetry, is negative. On the other hand, the warring of Abdiel and the loyal angels against Satan and his forces is approved in *Paradise Lost* because its cause is just.

Where Thersites had failed, Abdiel stands against the threats of Satan, denounces him before his followers a second time, escapes without harm, and is the first to strike Satan during the war. Thersites failed completely: he was given no further chance to reply to Odysseus who struck him into silent obedience with his truncheon. Thersites remains insignificant in the heroic world, while the Christian world of *Paradise Lost* allows heroism to the lowest of the angels because he is faithful to God. In order to stress this point even more, Milton placed Abdiel's two actions in the very center of the first edition of the epic, and, in spite of the later expansions, Abdiel remains central to the war in heaven. By his position in *Paradise Lost* and by the amount of space he is given, Abdiel has a greater significance than Thersites, but his earliest epic ancestor is still discernible.

Both poets use an inconspicuous character for the purpose of contrasting heroic and anti-heroic behavior. Hence the epic malcontents express the objections of the common soldiers to the glories of battle. The malcontents represent a widespread feeling that only they are courageous enough to utter. The Father, when He praises Abdiel, does not suggest that only he was faithful among the angels of the North but that only he publicly upheld 'Against revolted multitudes the Cause/ Of Truth' (VI, 31–2). Later Abdiel tells Satan that others also object to the rebellion:

> All are not of thy Train; there be who Faith
> Prefer, and Piety to God, though then
> To thee not visible, when I alone
> Seem'd in thy World erroneous to dissent
> From all: my Sect thou seest, now learn too late
> How few sometimes may know, when thousands err (VI, 143–8).

That many others have changed sides seems probable. This fact is not dwelled upon because it can be assumed in any battle narrative, and, more importantly, because Raphael wishes to stress to Adam what one common rebel can achieve when he acts in accordance with God's law. If a third of the angels, bound by fear and misled by the force and rhetoric of their leader, do remain and fall with Satan, as in the *Iliad*, the group psychology seems sound.

Milton not only classicized the obscure Abdiel; he also classicized Raphael, one of the traditional angels. Here the classical sources have not been neglected but the primacy of Virgil and the significance of Raphael's classical background have not been fully analyzed. Of those who recognize the close analogue to Virgil, Davis P. Harding and Thomas M. Greene, the first critic limits his investigation to Milton's wish to be compared with Virgil and Homer, while the second writer investigates Raphael's descent in relation to the archetype but does not examine its classical relevance.[3]

Milton developed Raphael through *retractatio*: Raphael's descent to earth, in style, structure, allusion, and episode, originates from Mercury's visit to Aeneas (*Aen*. IV, 219–80).[4] In Virgil, Jupiter sends Mercury to warn the hero not to prolong his stay in Carthage and reminds him of his Roman destiny. In spite of the brevity of this scene, Milton owes more to it than to any other classical source, though he has amplified and Christianized it. Like Mercury, Raphael is sent by the godhead to warn a hero against lethargy and the presence of enemies and to remind him that his destiny lies elsewhere; thus, the two visitors are signs of divine favor and dispensers of moral instruction.

Two ancient analogues often proposed and usually given equal authority with the Mercury episode occur in Homer. The first is Hermes' visit to Troy in the *Iliad* (XXIV, 333–470), during which he guides Priam safely through the Greek camp to Achilles' tent in order to obtain the body of Hector. Hermes' function is merely tutelary, however, not admonitory like that of Mercury and Raphael. Nor does he appear in his own shape, as the messengers do in Virgil and Milton, but assumes the guise of one of Achilles' retainers. Neither in form nor in content does the scene suggest the scene in *Paradise Lost*. In the second proposed source, Hermes is sent to spur the resumption of Odysseus' journey back to Ithaka (*Od.* V, 28–148). But Hermes does not confront Odysseus, only Calypso who is not morally instructed like Aeneas and Adam; she is asked only to submit to the will of Zeus by letting Odysseus leave Aiaia. Undoubtedly, these two Homeric scenes provided the basis for Virgil's episode, but they are only faintly echoed in Milton. Whatever details Milton derived from this scene, the main purpose and outline of Raphael's descent recall the earlier episode in the *Aeneid*, for it is the confrontation of the celestial and the earthly that forms the essence of the two scenes.

In that confrontation, Milton follows closely the structure and the thematic significance of Virgil's visit of Mercury. In both poems, the celestial descent is prompted by a prayer. In the *Aeneid*, Iarbas, the scorned suitor of Dido, prays to Jupiter to honor his sacrifice (IV, 206–18). Iarbas calls attention to his honorable offer of marriage to Dido, 'conubia nostra' (213), and the orthodoxy and sincerity of his religious practices, 'nos munera templis/quippe tuis ferimus' (217–18; 'indeed we are bringing gifts to your temples'). In *Paradise Lost*, Raphael is sent to Eden after, and perhaps because, Adam and Eve sing their 'unpremeditated' prayer on heavenly and earthly beauty. Raphael's descent seems also an answer to the narrator's request for someone to warn Adam and Eve of Satan's entrance into Eden:

> O for that warning voice, which he who saw
> Th' *Apocalypse* heard cry in Heav'n aloud,
> Then when the Dragon, put to second rout,
> Came furious down to be reveng'd on men,
> *Woe to the inhabitants on Earth!* that now,
> While time was, our first Parents had been warn'd
> The coming of their secret foe, and scap'd
> Haply so scap'd his mortal snare (IV, 1–8).

In both poems, the godhead responds by summoning a messenger to reprimand the hero's behavior. Jupiter commands Mercury to remind Aeneas that his destiny lies in Italy and not in Carthage, the future enemy of Rome. Aeneas, Jupiter claims, delays 'inimica in gente' (235; 'amidst a hostile people'). In the English epic, the Father tells Raphael to warn Adam of the presence of an enemy:

> tell him withal
> His danger, and from whom, what enemy
> Late fall'n himself from Heaven, is plotting now
> The fall of others from like state of bliss (V, 238–41).

If the summonings are alike, the journeys are even more so, since Milton's account of the descent from heaven follows Virgil's with less expansion than does his treatment of the rest of the angelic visit. But one major shift has occurred. Mercury began his journey by strapping on his sandals and taking up his wand. These instruments, Virgil tells us, give the god his power: with his wand, he can drive wind and clouds out of his way, and, with his sandals, he can fly over land and sea. With these instruments, Mercury opens the clouds that surround Olympus and flies to earth. Raphael possesses Mercury's powers without the apparatus required by his pagan counterpart. He too can fly over land and ocean and, because of the location of heaven, interstellar space. But Raphael is more a part of a community of spirits who cooperate to aid his flight. Mercury seemed to be alone, while Raphael is amidst a multitude who part to let him out of heaven: 'th' angelic Choirs/ On each hand parting, to his speed gave way/ Through all th' Empyreal road' (V, 251–3). Another aspect of celestial cooperation is the gates that open *sua sponte* for Raphael to pass out. These two actions correspond to Mercury's more traditional, magical exit. The contrast suits the purpose of Raphael's visit, for the angel is to be the guest of Adam and Eve whose social instincts he will help develop. He can help develop them because he too is part of a community that is closer to human society than the more severe hierarchy of Olympus. In this sense, heaven is closer to earth than to Olympus.

The juxtaposition of these two realms of life works in another way too, for the descent from heaven provides an opportunity to contrast the divine and the human conditions, an opportunity which neither poet neglects. To represent human life, Virgil presents a detailed description of Atlas, the mountain that supports the sky in Africa and upon which Mercury lands on his way to Carthage. Atlas is like an old man, bearded and weatherbeaten:

> iamque uolans apicem et latera ardua cernit
> Atlantis duri caelum qui uertice fulcit,
> Atlantis, cinctum adsidue cui nubibus atris
> piniferum caput et uento pulsatur et imbri,
> nix umeros infusa tegit, tum flumina mento
> praecipitant senis, et glacie riget horrida barba (IV, 246–51).

> (And now, flying he perceives the summit and steep sides of hard Atlas, who holds up the sky with his peak; Atlas, whose pine-bearing head is constantly girded about by dark clouds and beaten by wind and rain. The scattered snow covers his shoulders, while rivers rush from the chin of the old man and his bristling beard is hard with ice.)

Atlas, enduring the hardships of earthly existence, may be an image of the toiling Aeneas or just a representative of the hard lot of man that Virgil often pictures in the *Aeneid* and elsewhere. The ethereal messenger speeds by, stopping only momentarily, before he plunges to the sea: 'hic primum paribus nitens Cyllenius alis/constitit; hinc toto praeceps se corpore ad undas/misit' (IV,

252–4). The celestial is thus juxtaposed with the earthly. The latter is subject to suffering and to time; the former is almost beyond the limitations of time and space.

Milton too contrasts the heavenly and the terrestrial as he reports how clearly Raphael can see the earth from afar:

> From hence, no cloud, or, to obstruct his sight,
> Star interpos'd, however small he sees,
> Not unconform to other shining Globes,
> Earth and the Gard'n of God, with Cedars crown'd
> Above all Hills (V, 257–61).

Milton employs similes to heighten the contrast. Through these similes, alluding to Galileo and the pilot on the Aegean, we are reminded of fallen man's weak vision, as he looks back to the source of life:

> As when by night the Glass
> Of *Galileo*, less assur'd, observes
> Imagin'd Lands and Regions of the Moon:
> Or Pilot from amidst the *Cyclades*
> *Delos* or *Samos* first appearing kens
> A cloudy spot (V, 261–6).

Such contrasts are appropriate, since both messengers will present warnings which emphasize the vulnerability of, hence the inferiority of, human in relation to divine natures. For that reason, the celestial message should be heeded. To the reader, this divine preeminence illuminates the error of not following the divine will, since the divinity is beyond space and time and knows the future. As the deity willingly imparts this knowledge to man to correct his ways, heaven is also beneficent. To reject such celestial advice is to be unwise and ungrateful.

Besides such structural and thematic similarities, Milton also recalls Virgil by a series of verbal echoes from the *Aeneid*. In the passages that deal with Raphael and Adam, these echoes are more explicitly Virgilian than Milton's normal Latinate mode of expression. When Milton compares Raphael to 'Maia's son' (V, 285), he is translating Virgil's epithet for Mercury, 'Maia genitum' (*Aen*. I, 297).[5] This phrase appears when the god is sent to assure the safe entrance of Aeneas into Carthage. Though the Virgilian context is not relevant to Raphael's task, the phrase would most likely suggest the later passage in Virgil that we have been discussing, since the whole episode involving Raphael follows closely the later descent of Jove's messenger. This suggestion would be strengthened by three other Virgilian echoes which definitely derive from this later descent of Mercury. The first is when Milton writes 'Down thither prone in flight/ He speeds' (V, 266–7) which, in syntax and in vocabulary, recalls Virgil's words 'hinc toto praeceps se corpore ad undas/misit' (IV, 253–4). The second phrase is 'Winnows the buxom Air' (V, 270) which has its source in 'uentosque secabat' (IV, 257). The third echo is Adam's referring to Raphael as the 'Divine Interpreter' (VII, 72), which recalls Aeneas' description of Mercury as 'interpres diuum' (IV, 378).

Milton does more than echo Virgil's descent of Mercury, however. Though he always works close to the earlier passage, he expands, substitutes, and rechannels the elements in the *Aeneid* to fit his Christian theme. For instance, Virgil compares Mercury in flight to a bird, 'aui similis' (IV, 254), who flies about the rocky coasts of Africa, while Milton expands the simile and makes it more specific by using the image of the phoenix to describe the flight of Raphael:

> to all the Fowls he seems
> A *Phoenix*, gaz'd by all, as that sole Bird
> When to enshrine his reliques in the Sun's
> Bright Temple, to *Egyptian Thebes* he flies (V, 271–4).

Virgil's simile stresses the lowly flight of the bird, perhaps in search of fish: 'quae circum litora, circum/piscosos scopulos humilis uolat aequora iuxta' (IV, 254–5; 'who flies low about the shores and about the rocks surrounded by fish, close to the sea's surface'). This humble comparison Milton turns into the phoenix, a symbol of immortality and perhaps a reminder of the sacrifice of Christ on the cross.[6]

Another such amplification and Christianization lies in the physical description of Raphael. Raphael's counterpart has wings but Virgil gives no detailed account of them. Presumably, Mercury has wings on his 'talaria,' his sandals, which are often pictured in classical art. In *Paradise Lost*, Raphael has six wings, like the seraphim in Isaiah (VI: 2), painted in silver, gold, 'colors dipt in Heav'n,' and 'Sky-tinctur'd grain.' Mercury is given no colorful attire, but Aeneas significantly is: Mercury finds Aeneas wearing a jasper sword and a cloak of Tyrian purple threaded with gold. The sword about his waist is 'stellatus' so that he resembles Raphael, who is 'Girt like a Starry Zone':

atque illi stellatus iaspide fulua
ensis erat Tyrioque ardebat murice laena
demissa ex umeris, diues quae munera Dido
fecerat, et tenui telas discreuerat auro (IV, 261–4).

(And he had a sword starred with yellow jasper and a cloak hung from his shoulders blazed with Tyrian purple, gifts which rich Dido had made and had woven the threads with fine gold.)

In the *Aeneid*, these colors characterize the gifts of Dido who keeps Aeneas in Carthage, away from the founding of Rome. Hence, they are suggestive of slackness and effeminacy. In *Paradise Lost*, such signs of splendor are appropriately transferred to the inhabitant of heaven, who wears them as emblems of God's glory.

But a more important shift has taken place between the celestial messenger and his listener: the relationship between the human and the divine has changed as well. Mercury produces terror in Aeneas, who remains speechless and anxious to flee, after Mercury has delivered his message: 'At uero Aeneas aspectu obmutuit amens,/arrectaeque horrore comae et uox faucibus haesit./ardet abire fuga dulcisque relinquere terras' (IV, 279–81; 'And indeed Aeneas became silent, distracted at the sight, and his hair stood up in fright and his voice clung to his throat. He burns to take flight and leave those pleasant lands'). Mercury reminds Aeneas of the power that Jupiter has over men and speaks like a superior to him. Adam and Raphael are on different terms. They share a meal and spend the rest of the day listening to one another giving accounts of the past. Although Raphael is clearly the superior being, he diminishes the distance between heaven and earth by suggesting that earth may be the shadow of heaven, by explaining that angels love in some way analogous to the way human beings do, by partaking of human food, and by giving Adam neo-Platonic instructions on how man can attain the angelic level of being: 'time may come when men/ With Angels may participate' (V, 493–4). Even when he warns Adam against uxoriousness, Raphael is firm, but never terrifying. The human exists only a little below the divine in Milton, at least before the fall. Afterwards, man's powers lapse; he falls away from the celestial. Aeneas, from Milton's viewpoint, would be in that fallen state.

The changes aside, the major similarity between the two scenes lies in the messages of Mercury and Raphael. Even though the angel's words are an expansion and Christianization of Mercury's, their Virgilian origins are not obscured. Mercury's speech consists in one short message:

> 'tu nunc Karthaginis altae
> fundamenta locas pulchramque uxorius urbem
> exstruis? heu, regni rerumque oblite tuarum!
> ipse deum tibi me claro demittit Olympo
> regnator, caelum et terras qui numine torquet,
> ipse haec ferre iubet celeris mandata per auras:
> quid struis? aut qua spe Libycis teris otia terris?
> si te nulla mouet tantarum gloria rerum
> [nec super ipse tua moliris laude laborem,]
> Ascanium surgentem et spes heredis Iuli
> respice, cui regnum Italiae Romanaque tellus
> debetur' (IV, 265–76).

> ('Do you now place the foundations of high Carthage and build a beautiful city, enslaved by a wife? Alas! You have forgotten your kingdom and your business! The ruler of the gods himself sends me down from bright Olympus, he who turns heaven and earth with his will. He himself bids me carry these commands through the swift winds: what are you thinking of? Or in what hope do you wear out your leisure in Libyan lands? If no glory of great deeds moves you nor do you yourself besides undertake any labor for future fame, consider the growing Ascanius and the hopes of your heir Iulus, to whom an Italian kingdom and a Roman land are due.')

A keynote for the passage is struck by the word 'uxorius,' its Latin meaning in this instance corresponding to its English cognate. The same word, 'uxorius hic,' was used to describe Adam in *De Doctrina Christiana*, wherein Milton was following the Augustinian tradition of making Adam subordinate to his mate.[7] The same conception of Adam is present in Milton's epic. Adam explains his potentially uxorious affection for Eve to his interlocutor:

> yet when I approach
> Her loveliness, so absolute she seems
> And in herself complete, so well to know
> Her own, that what she wills to do or say,
> Seems wisest, virtuousest, discreetest, best;
> All higher knowledge in her presence falls
> Degraded, Wisdom in discourse with her
> Loses discount'nanc't, and like folly shows (VIII, 546–53).

Lest Adam allow passion to sway his rational judgment, Raphael rebukes him for uxoriousness:

> For what admir'st thou, what transports thee so,
> An outside? fair no doubt, and worthy well
> Thy cherishing, thy honoring, and thy love,
> Not thy subjection: weigh with her thyself;
> Then value (VIII, 567–71).

Besides being criticized for uxoriousness, Aeneas is rebuked for neglecting his duty to his son, his race, and his destiny: 'heu, regni rerumque oblite tuarum' (IV, 267). The hero is neglecting the will of Jove and fate in favor of human passion. Aeneas must found a greater city because Carthage is doomed to destruction; hence it is mortal and earthly, while Rome will be eternal (even if fraught with human frailty). In the same way, Raphael reminds Adam of a higher good, a purer love, that is incompatible with human passion: 'In loving thou dost well, in passion not,/ Wherein true Love consists not; Love refines/ The thoughts' (VIII, 588–90). Both Mercury and Raphael call for a higher goal than human passion. For the Roman poet, that goal is the future empire and another, more fitting bride for Aeneas, Lavinia. In both poems, man is warned against being enslaved by the beloved and misled by emotion. Adam's love for Eve must be tempered by reason; he must keep in mind the higher good which ultimately is love of God, while Aeneas must place the future empire above his affection for Dido. Each hero has a goal which is represented by a place. Raphael urges Adam, as Mercury urged Aeneas, to think of another, more fit place of habitation. Adam's new abode is a state of mind which, as Raphael explains, will transform his body and give him entrance to more ethereal realms:

> Your bodies may at last turn all to spirit,
> Improv'd by tract of time, and wing'd ascend
> Ethereal, as wee, or may at choice
> Here or in Heav'nly Paradises dwell (V, 497–500).

To make their messages more forceful, both god and angel remind their hearers that they are divine emissaries. Mercury reminds Aeneas of Jupiter's power which turns heaven and earth: 'ipse deum tibi me claro demittit Olympo/regnator, caelum et terras qui numine torquet' (IV, 268–9). In *Paradise Lost*, Raphael presents Adam with an account of Creation as well as an account of the war in heaven. The Creation story, though an immediate answer to Adam's questions about the universe, serves to impress upon Adam the power and glory of God, just as the account of the war in heaven also serves to reinforce Adam's conception of God's might. Such accounts lend authority to Raphael's later admonitions in the way that Mercury's briefer statement impresses itself on the frightened Aeneas.

Most importantly, both speeches emphasize the need to be active, to follow the commands of the divinity, and to improve one's self. Mercury appeals to the epic reward of glory which should excite the hero out of his 'otium' on to the achievement of great deeds. His reward shall be praise, 'tua moliris laude laborem' (IV, 273), if Aeneas will only change his ways. Milton, working in a Christian context, can offer more. Raphael explains in neo-Platonic terms how man must work at self perfection, so that 'corporeal to incorporeal' may turn (V, 413). Mercury can offer no such reward, but he can promise the pagan consolation of eternal fame as a spur to selflessness: Aeneas is called to search for something immortal and to abandon the ephemeral. Likewise, Adam is asked to look toward the eternal; he must try to elevate himself above the material and the imperfect.

When both celestial messengers conclude their speeches, they appeal not just to the heroes themselves, but urge them to consider their future offspring. Mercury tells Aeneas that Ascanius was promised an Italian kingdom and a Roman land which Aeneas should bequeath, as an immortal kingdom, to his son: 'Ascanium surgentem et spes heredis Iuli/respice, cui regnum Italiae Romanaque tellus/debetur' (IV, 274–6). Raphael makes a similar appeal to Adam: passion must not interfere with man's spiritual growth nor with his abode in Eden, because to the sons of Adam are due an inheritance of virtue:

> take heed lest Passion sway
> Thy judgment to do aught, which else free Will
> Would not admit; thine and of all thy Sons
> The weal or woe in thee is plac'd; beware (VIII, 635–8).

Adam's actions involve the whole of mankind, while Aeneas' affect only his immediate descendants. But Aeneas is to found a kingdom that, according to Anchises in the underworld, shall bring universal peace and justice to the whole world (VI, 852–3) so his too is a general destiny. What is missing in Virgil is the personal immortality conferred by Christianity.

Otherwise, Milton echoes closely the descent of Mercury to

Aeneas, in style, structure, and content. In his language, Milton reminds us, more often than usual, of Virgil, some phrases being actually translations from the *Aeneid*. The pattern of prayer, the sending of the messenger, the journey to earth, the imagery, the contrast of human and divine powers, and the message itself repeat the sequence of events originated by the Roman poet. Furthermore, both Mercury and Raphael adjure their hearers to put aside earthly passion, to act in accordance with the divine will, and to look to a higher mode of life. Though the passage from Virgil has been expanded and Christianized, the similarities invite the reader familiar with the *Aeneid* to see how *Paradise Lost* has given the Biblical story epic dignity by building upon Virgil and how the Christian epic complements and fulfills the pagan epic and how Milton has become the English Virgil.

Raphael also helps to sort out a pagan theological error. When he descends to earth he unfastidiously eats the food and drinks the wine of earth. In the *Iliad*, we are expressly told by Homer that the gods do not eat food or drink wine (V, 341) and when Hermes descends in the *Odyssey* he eats ambrosia and drinks nectar (V, 92–5). Milton's point in this small part of the epic dialogue is important: Raphael follows his demonstration of the angelic appetite by telling Adam that men may rise to the level of angels some day: 'time may come when men/ With Angels may participate' (V, 493–4). The possibility of man's perfecting himself is only possible if Adam realizes that the difference between men and angels is quantitative and not qualitative. As Raphael tells Adam: reason has two forms, 'Discursive' and 'Intuitive; discourse/ Is oftest yours, the latter most is ours,/ Differing but in degree, of kind the same' (V, 488–90). Prelapsarian man is closer to divinities than the fallen man of the Homeric epics, since Homer's gods had the advantage of immortality over men, but that is only because Homer saw with a false light: men may perhaps even now become gods, since all are nourished by the same Creator.

Often, in *Paradise Lost*, the angels take over the positive functions of various epic characters, such as Abdiel's opposition and Raphael's warning. The angels correct or expand upon their classical parallels; sometimes they do both. A good example of the latter is Raphael's account of creation. The reader of classical epic has met nothing of this elaborate treatment of the origins of the world in classical epic; only the accounts of Lucretius and Ovid come to mind at first. But if we read Milton in close conjunction with classical epic, we may recall, as did J. A. K. Thomson,[8] Iopas' song of creation in the *Aeneid*. His account is short and vague:

> cithara crinitus Iopas
> personat aurata, docuit quem maximus Atlas.
> hic canit errantem lunam solisque labores,
> unde hominum genus et pecudes, unde imber et ignes,
> Arcturum pluuiasque Hyadas geminosque Triones,
> quid tantum Oceano properent se tingere soles
> hiberni, uel quae tardis mora noctibus obstet (I, 740–6).
>
> (. . . long haired Iopas makes the hall ring with his golden lyre, Iopas whom great Atlas taught. He sings of the wandering moon and the labors of the sun, of the origins of the human race and of beasts, of the source of rain and fire, and of Arcturus, the rainy Hyades, and the twin bears, and why the winter suns so hasten to immerse themselves in the ocean or what delay hinders the slow nights.)

T. E. Page reminds us that Homer's bards sang of war, a tradition that Virgil changed in this passage: his bard sings of philosophy.[9] Milton expands Virgil's passage of a few lines to a whole book (VII) and adds a theological dimension that is missing in the account of Iopas. The same kind of displacement occurs when Michael expands and changes Anchises' account of history; what takes Anchises less than 150 lines (VI, 756–892) takes Michael two books (XI and XII). Milton is using the full weight of biblical philosophy and history to outstrip his predecessors.

The angels are also superior warriors in the style of the *Iliad* and the *Aeneid*. Abdiel, Gabriel, and Michael all have their 'aristeiai' (moments of glory) on the battlefield. They wield victorious swords and wear armor like their classical counterparts. Even when Satan cannonades them, they still remain classical warriors: 'They pluckt the seated Hills with all their load,/ Rocks, Waters, Woods, and by the shaggy tops/ Uplifting bore them in thir hands' (VI, 644–6). These rocky hills are the culmination in epic poetry of what we might call 'the epic stone,' which is used to show the degeneration of man and the great strength of the epic heroes. In the *Iliad* (XII, 445–62), Hector smashes the gates of the Greek camp with a stone which two men of the present, the poet assures us, could not lift at all, though Zeus helps Hector lift it. Virgil excells Homer by having Turnus lift a stone that twelve men could not lift, men of the sort that exist now, without any divine help (XII, 896–900). No doubt Milton's angels have divine help in the righteousness of their cause. If the men of today are degenerate, compared to the heroes of the classical epic, those heroes themselves are distinctly inferior to the angelic warriors that preceded them, the hurlers of rocky mountains.[10]

The loyal angels often resemble their disobedient counterparts, as when both groups indulge in epic games: the followers of Satan (II, 528–46) and the guardians of paradise (IV, 551–2). It is not the classical convention that is evil – games are the necessary practice for war – but the orientation of the spirit: towards God or towards the self. The loyal angels act as agents of God, not as classical heroes trying to gain immortality through glorious action:

> At which command the Powers Militant,
> That stood for Heav'n, in mighty Quadrate join'd
> Of Union irresistible, mov'd on
> In silence thir bright Legions, to the sound
> Of instrumental Harmony that breath'd
> Heroic Ardor to Advent'rous deeds
> Under thir God-like Leaders, in the Cause
> Of God and his *Messiah* (VI, 61–8).

It is the inner harmony that produces this 'Heroic Ardor,' the harmony that proceeds from obedience to God. When peace returns, they do not sing, like the rebel angels, 'Thir own Heroic deeds' (II, 549), but the praises of the Son and the Father:

> Hail Son of God, Savior of Men, thy Name
> Shall be the copious matter of my Song
> Henceforth, and never shall my Harp thy praise
> Forget, nor from thy Father's praise disjoin (III, 412–15).

The Son is a worthy recipient of heroic song, for He too, as well as the angels, is truly heroic in both the Christian and the classical sense of that term and Milton portrayed Him as such, as Vida had done in his *Christiad* (1535) and Milton himself had done earlier when he praised the heroic action of the Son in 'The Passion' with his own harp:

> For now to sorrow must I tune my song,
> And set my Harp to notes of saddest woe,
> Which on our dearest Lord did seize ere long,
> Dangers, and snares, and wrongs and worse than so,
> Which he for us did freely undergo:
>   Most perfect *Hero*, tried in heaviest plight
> Of labors huge and hard, too hard for human wight (8–14).

When we meet the Son in *Paradise Lost*, he has been thoroughly acclimatized to the epic poem. He does not resemble the figure on the cross that we find in the Bible or the man of Galilee that we find in *Paradise Regained*. He appears in the longer epic in two primary roles: that of intercessor and that of heroic warrior.

When the Son offers his life for man, we find no epic similes and no direct allusions to classical epic; yet the scene remains classical as well as biblical. The classical parallels begun earlier in the poem do not stop but shift to a higher plane: the classical pattern is there but further in the background, because the Son rises so far above his epic predecessors. Formally the scene in heaven is familiar as a council on Olympus, a council that appears in all three major classical epics. As we recall these scenes, we can see the general background behind Milton's heavenly council (*contaminatio*). In each classical epic, someone successfully intercedes for man with the godhead. In the *Iliad*, Thetis appeals to Zeus to help Achilles by punishing the Greeks. Although her request is granted, it causes the death of Achilles' beloved Patroklos; thus her request precipitates the tragedy of the poem. Zeus, we begin to see through Milton's retreatment of the scene, is unable to save men; he only has the power to destroy them. Later Zeus weeps tears of blood because he is unable to save his own son, Sarpedon. Fate rules the Homeric world so that Apollo must leave Hector's side when it is time for the hero to be killed. In the *Aeneid*, Venus intercedes for Aeneas in a scene Virgil constructed to echo the scene between Thetis and Zeus in the *Iliad*. Jupiter tells Venus that fate will save Aeneas: ' "parce metu, Cytherea, manent immota tuorum/fata tibi" ' (I, 257–8; ' "Do not fear, Venus, the fate of your children remains unchanged" '). Destiny in the *Aeneid* is in accord with Aeneas and the Trojans, while, in the *Iliad*, destiny is against Achilles, Hector, and the Trojans. Like the other two epics, the *Odyssey* has an intercession of a goddess for a mortal in its first book also. Athene successfully requests help for Odysseus' return to Ithaka. Zeus grants her request partly out of affection for Odysseus and partly out of admiration for his virtuous behavior (I, 64–79). In the *Odyssey*, we find more a sense of justice both in this scene and throughout the rest of the poem. But fate seems to be in control in the *Odyssey* too; else Poseidon would have destroyed Odysseus for the blinding of Polyphemos. In any case, Athene cannot save Odysseus from the death which is foretold by Teiresias (XI, 119–37). The same prophecy of the death of the hero is made by Jupiter to Venus

(*Aen.* I, 265) and by Thetis to Achilles (*Il.* I, 416). But none of these intercessors can offer their lives to save man. Only the Son rescues man from the mortality that he cannot escape in the classical epic.

The second major role that the Son adopts in *Paradise Lost*, that of warrior, has been noticed by Steadman; I wish to add, and analyze His relationship to, the prototype.[11] As warrior as well as intercessor, He carries on the image of Athene. Like her, the Son rushes into battle with his Father's chariot and wields His thunderbolt. If Athene carries the aegis of Zeus with the head of the Gorgon on it (V, 733–91) when she descends to battle, the Gorgon is now replaced by the cherubs of the Son's Chariot of Paternal Deity. But the image is transformed so that the classical chariot of Zeus blends into the chariot of Ezekiel. It is the best example in *Paradise Lost* of *ekphrasis* (description of a work of art), but this time artifice serves God, not man:

> The Chariot of Paternal Deity,
> Flashing thick flames, Wheel within Wheel, undrawn,
> Itself instinct with Spirit, but convoy'd
> By four Cherubic shapes, four faces each
> Had wondrous, as with Stars thir bodies all
> And Wings were set with Eyes, with Eyes the Wheels
> Of Beryl, and careering Fires between;
> Over thir heads a crystal Firmament,
> Whereon a Sapphire Throne, inlaid with pure
> Amber, and colors of the show'ry Arch.
> Hee in Celestial Panoply all arm'd
> Of radiant *Urim*, work divinely wrought,
> Ascended, at his right hand Victory
> Sat Eagle-wing'd, beside him hung his Bow
> And Quiver with three-bolted Thunder stor'd
> And from about him fierce Effusion roll'd
> Of smoke and bickering flame, and sparkles dire;
> Attended with ten thousand thousand Saints (VI, 750–67).

Athene's chariot seems a dim and mistaken reflection of the true chariot of the godhead, yet both within their spheres accomplish similar tasks. The Greek epic recalled the flying and flaming chariot, but Milton has now displaced it with its true source (Ezek. I: 4–26) and all beauty and all power are handed over to God.

The Son emerges from the battle in heaven as the archetype of the classical warrior, just as Satan was his distortion. The Son, no longer the humble and self-sacrificing intercessor of the council in heaven, is the true Achilles. Here real displacement occurs. The wrath of Achilles has become the wrath of God: 'His count'nance too severe to be beheld/ And full of wrath bent on his Enemies' (VI, 825–6). The vengeance that Achilles arrogated to himself is no longer acceptable in the epic poem: 'Vengeance is his, or whose he sole appoints' (VI, 808), as the Son says of the Father. The rapid assimilation of Achillean powers, his easy defeat of his enemies, and his dependence upon the Father's power has changed the *mores* of the classical battlefield: power has been centralized in God and taken away from man. Ironically the self-sacrificing Son is at once a greater warrior than Achilles and a more merciful one. The Son stops pursuing his enemies although Achilles went on killing mercilessly till he learned humility. The war in heaven, played off against a Homeric background which it dwarfs, has replaced the Trojan War as the most important battle in epic poetry.

The war in heaven, like everything else in this theocentric epic, leads back to the Father and to Him we now turn. In spite of the many writers who have shared the theocentric notion of the world with Milton, startlingly few have attempted to represent Him in their work. The one poet whom we might have expected to make a representation of the Father ends his *Divine Comedy* with the mystical emblem of the rose. The medieval dramatists hardly ever gave the Father more than a walk-on part, and later writers give us only glimpses of Him, as in Tasso and Goethe. The reasons for this omission are not difficult to find: besides the imaginative hardships of trying to create a concrete image of a being beyond our ken, the Bible does not present us with a concrete picture, unless we are content to see the godhead as the jealous God of the Hebrews. While the Son has a clearly delineated personality from the New Testament, the Father has remained outside the grasp of literature for the most part, and so a writer must risk creating a deity on his own. Milton's creation then was a bold one and has left a lively controversy behind it, but, without investigating various reactions to Milton's deity, I shall investigate the Father only in relation to his classical archetype, which has gone unnoticed.[12]

Although Milton had little precedent in epic poetry for the treatment of the Christian godhead, he solved the difficulty in the same manner as Michelangelo solved it in art. Michelangelo fastened biblical faces onto the heroic statues of the classical era.

His studies of the Torso Belvedere and other classical statues helped him to merge Christian and pagan art, thereby giving Christianity the stature of classical heroism – the same process that Milton was applying to the epic poem.[13] Such a merging was the greatest proof that Milton did not reject the classical epic *in toto* but even made his deity partly classical.

Equating Zeus and the Father through theocrasia was a commonplace of the Renaissance. It is a frequent commonplace in Milton's poetry: in *Lycidas*, Apollo speaks of 'all-judging *Jove*,' as the ruler of heaven (82), the attendant Spirit in *Comus* tells us that he was sent 'by quick command from Sovran *Jove*' (41), and his counterpart in the 'Arcades,' Genius, derives his power 'from *Jove*' (44), as does the nightingale in the first sonnet (7).

In *Paradise Lost*, we find a sifting out of the pagan truths about the godhead. The falsehoods must be rejected. The amusing domestic bickering that we find in Homer's scenes between Zeus and Hera must be eliminated. As Milton wrote in *An Apology Against a Pamphlet*, Homer was said 'to have written undecent things of the gods' (*Prose*, I, 891). Milton is also bound by theological restrictions, such as the power of God over fate, but, in spite of restrictions, Milton uses allusion, structure, and style to lead us back to Olympus. No doubt he soars above the Olympian mount, but we can still see it below him.

Milton's God dwells in a heaven where we find the 'Holy Mount' (V, 712) which emits the odor of ambrosia (II, 245; III, 135), reminiscent of Olympus, and the river, running through heaven 'o'er *Elesian* flowers' (III, 359) which corresponds to the Eridanus, running through Virgil's Elysian Fields (*Aen.* VI, 659).

The Father Himself is even more solidly linked to the classical epic tradition. Sometimes the allusions are indirect, as when we are told that the architect of Pandemonium is Mulciber, 'thrown by angry *Jove*/ Sheer o'er the Crystal Battlements' (I, 741–2), thus equating God with Zeus, who hurled Mulciber, or Hephaistos, out of heaven (*Il.* I, 590–4). More often the parallel is developed by *retractatio* or *contaminatio*. By these last two methods especially, Milton compares and contrasts the omniscience, the omnipotence, the sympathy, and the justice of Jove and the Father.

When Milton's God demonstrates His omniscience, the epic tradition, which has been invoked throughout the poem, reminds us of the similarity of godheads in epic poetry. The Father, when He first appears in *Paradise Lost*, plays the role of prophet, foretelling the fall of man: 'So will fall/ Hee and his faithless Progeny' (III, 95–6). The manner of His prophecy, the epic council scene, and its style, the relatively unadorned language of direct speech, lead us to the classical epic. The God of the Bible does not speak with the same directness but resorts to prophets. The father of the gods, as Homer and Virgil present him, appears in his own person, in council, and prophesies the outcome of the epic and the cause of that outcome. So Zeus in the *Iliad* pronounces:

> *'τὸν δὲ κτενεῖ ἔγχεϊ φαίδιμος Ἕκτωρ*
> *Ἰλίου προπάροιθε, πολέας ὀλέσαντ' αἰζηοὺς*
> *τοὺς ἄλλους μετὰ δ' υἱὸν ἐμὸν Σαρπηδόνα δῖον.*
> *τοῦ δὲ χολωσάμενος κτενεῖ Ἕκτορα δῖος Ἀχιλλεύς'* (XV, 65–8).

> ('shining Hector will kill him [Patroklos] with his spear before Troy after he has destroyed many other vigorous men, including my son, glorious Sarpedon. In rage for him, glorious Achilles will kill Hector.')

Likewise in the *Odyssey*, Zeus forecasts Odysseus' successful return to Ithaka (I, 77–9) – I have already commented on Jupiter's forecast of Aeneas' success in Italy. This power of prophecy is extended beyond the scope of the epic plot by secondary prophets in all epics. The death of Achilles has already been mentioned and so has the death of Odysseus, these prophecies being delegated to Thetis and Teiresias respectively, while the future of Rome is projected by Anchises and the future of the human race by Michael. The view of history, of course, widens as we approach the end of the epic tradition.

If Milton's God rivals Zeus in omniscience, He excells him in power. Zeus bows to fate in the *Iliad* when Hera reminds him that if he interferes with it he will set a bad precedent. Zeus wishes to save Sarpedon and to contradict fate but learns from Hera that the other gods also have sons on the battlefield whom they will want to save, so he yields (XVI, 440–9, cf. XXII, 178–81). This ambiguity of the source of power continues in the classical epic.[14] In the *Iliad*, Zeus yields the option of countermanding fate out of weakness. In the *Odyssey* and the *Aeneid*, the question does not arise because the will of god accords with that of fate, but the ambiguity exists, as in Helenus' prophecy to Aeneas where both powers exist side by side:

> 'Nate dea (nam te maioribus ire per altum
> auspiciis manifesta fides; sic fata deum rex

> sortitur uoluitque uices, is uertitur ordo),
> pauca tibi e multis, quo tutior hospita lustres
> aequora et Ausonio possis considere portu,
> expediam dictis; prohibent nam cetera Parcae
> scire Helenum farique uetat Saturnia Iuno' (III, 374–80).
>
> ('Goddess born (for there is clear proof that you pass through the sea with higher auspices; thus the king of the gods distributes the fates and wheels about changes, and the course of events unrolls), I shall reveal a few words to you out of many, so that you can more safely traverse the strange seas and settle in an Italian port; for the Fates forbid Helenus to know more and Saturnian Juno forbids me to speak.')

The mystery of fate served Satan well when he had to rouse his troops in hell, but the idea is dispelled in *Paradise Lost*, when the Father bluntly states, 'Necessity and Chance/ Approach not mee, and what I will is Fate' (VII, 172–3). Indirectly the Father reminds us of the original meaning of 'fatum,' 'that which is said' (from L. 'for'), pointing out the philological truth behind the theological one: fate is the word of God.

The Father not only possesses Zeus' power and more, but His power is often presented in terms of the classical deity, as if Zeus were a partial reflection of the Christian God. The golden chain that hangs from heaven in the *Iliad*, the chain by which Zeus claims to be able to haul all the gods and Mount Olympus up into the air (VIII, 19–27), now hangs beneath the floor of heaven. Satan sees this chain of Zeus as he flies to earth,[15] the chain being an ironic reminder of the true source of the power of the classical world that Satan is now arrogating to himself. Zeus claimed only the power to raise up Olympus, or the planet (the Homeric text is ambiguous), but from Milton's heaven hangs the whole solar universe: 'And fast by hanging in a golden Chain/ This pendant world, in bigness as a Star/ Of smallest Magnitude close by the Moon' (II, 1051–3; cf. II, 1005).

We have already seen Milton's God as the power behind the Son's success on the battlefield. The Father makes an effective contrast with Zeus whose powers on the battlefield are less effective than those of many of the other gods and goddesses. Zeus may wield the thunderbolt on occasion, but usually he is passive during the contest on the field. The dramatic intervention of the Father in the war ends the conflict, while Zeus usually helplessly watches the battles from the top of Olympus. When he allows Hera and Athene to take the chariot to Troy, it is with reluctance: Zeus gives up his support for the Trojans and lets Athene lure Hector to his death. On the other hand, the Father is in complete control of fate and ends the war by delegating his chariot to the Son who sweeps his enemies out of heaven. The Father's chariot being omnipotent, Zeus' chariot appears weak by contrast. Such is Milton's use of *retractatio* to show the power of the Christian deity.

Milton also employs *contaminatio*. When Satan and Gabriel are about to fight in Eden, the scales appear in the sky:

> Th' Eternal to prevent such horrid fray
> Hung forth in Heav'n his golden Scales, yet seen
> Betwixt *Astrea* and the *Scorpion* sign,
> Wherein all things created first he weigh'd,
> The pendulous round Earth with balanc'd Air
> In counterpoise, now ponders all events,
> Battles and Realms: in these he put two weights
> The sequel each of parting and of fight;
> The latter quick up flew, and kickt the beam (IV, 996–1004).

When Zeus weighs the fate of Greeks and Trojans in the scales (*Il.* VIII, 69–72), we do not know whether he is demonstrating his support for the Trojans or trying to learn what fate has in store, but when he balances in the scales the life and death of Hector, it seems that he is learning if now is the time for Hector's death. In Virgil, there is no ambiguity when Jupiter weighs the fates of Turnus and Aeneas, since the subjunctive of an indirect question tells us that Jupiter is seeking an answer, 'quem damnet labor et quo uergat pondere letum' (XII, 727; 'which one the struggle destroys and by which weight destruction inclines'). Milton associates the scales with the will of God, which is further associated with justice in the figure of Astrea. Setting God behind the movements of celestial bodies was a commonplace in the Renaissance, but Milton has conflated these earlier epic precedents into this scene. As Dryden noticed, Milton has reversed the scales both of Homer and of Virgil.[16] The reason is apparently to emphasize the shift from a classical to a Christian perspective. In the classical epic, the sinking scale means defeat, while in Milton the lighter scale does. Gabriel glosses the text:

> *Satan*, I know thy strength, and thou know'st mine,
> Neither our own but giv'n; what folly then
> To boast what Arms can do, since thine no more
> Than Heav'n permits, nor mine, though doubl'd now

To trample thee as mire: for proof look up,
And read thy Lot in yon celestial Sign (IV, 1006–11).

The appearance of the will of God in the sky does not balance the fates of the two warriors, but, as Verity notes, shows whether there should be a fight at all; hence the scales are a Christian rejection of hybristic heroism in general, represented by Satan, for he and Gabriel confront each other in very Homeric poses of flyting and brandishing of spears. The difficulties of the relationship between fate and the will of God, a vexing question for modern, but not ancient, readers of the classical epics – for they never conceived of the question in quite those terms – are solved in *Paradise Lost* and exemplified by a classical motif that demonstrates the truth of the Father's assertion, 'what I will is Fate' (VII, 173).

Milton's God excells Zeus further by turning the degenerate classicism of Satan to good. The degenerate classical values of hell approach earth in the form of Sin and Death who are turned into harbingers of degenerate antiquity by some of the heaviest use of classical myth in the poem. Homeric similes increase and in one case prefigure the commonly dreaded image of the battlefield strewn with unburied corpses:

So saying, with delight he snuff'd the smell
Of mortal change on Earth. As when a flock
Of ravenous Fowl, though many a League remote,
Against the day of Battle, to a Field,
Where Armies lie encampt, come flying, lur'd
With scent of living Carcasses design'd
For death, the following day, in bloody fight (X, 272–8).

The picture might well suggest that of the opening of the *Iliad* where the poet tells of the corpses left prey to the birds and the dogs, corpses killed by Achilles in his wrath (I, 3–5). But the birds of prey in *Paradise Lost* are not the random scavengers of the *Iliad*, they are the unwitting servants of God: they

know not that I call'd and drew them thither
My Hell-hounds, to lick up the draff and filth
Which man's polluting Sin with taint hath shed
On what was pure (X, 629–32).

Death may carry the trident of Poseidon and possess the power of the Gorgon (X, 293–7), but this classicism, perverted as it is, is doing the work of God, cleaning up the work of man's original sin. Just like their counterparts, Sleep and Death, who carry off the dead Sarpedon in the *Iliad* under orders from Zeus (*Il*. XVI, 454; 672), Sin and Death are in the service of the godhead. The text almost glosses the opening of the *Iliad* where Homer, after calling up the picture of the corpse-strewn battlefield, adds '*Διὸς δ' ἐτελείτο βουλή*' (I, 5; 'Thus the will of Zeus was accomplished'). It is as if Milton were correcting Homer in the light of Christianity by revealing the Father behind the common classical picture of death and showing that it was always the punishment for man's sin and that death was always in the service of God, who triumphs over Zeus by controlling and conquering death itself.

As Milton's God resembles and excells Zeus in power, he resembles and excells him in righteous anger.[17] In the *Iliad*, the only classical epic that shows Zeus often in bad temper, the father of the gods directs his anger at Hera for the most part, or at the other gods who participate in the war (VIII, 5–27). His anger does not usually correspond to the demands of justice. In one instance it does: when Zeus '*θυμὸν ἐνὶ στήθεσσιν ἀνῆκεν*' (*Il*. XVI, 691; 'drove rage into the heart') of Patroklos, as a fit punishment for his presumption on the battlefield. Zeus drives Patroklos on, as the Father drives on hardened sinners, 'But hard be hard'n'd, blind be blinded more,/ That they may stumble on, and deeper fall' (III, 200–1). The Father makes use of *ἄτη*, the destructive blindness that Zeus sends to evil over-reachers and that the Father in the Old Testament sends into the heart of Pharaoh (Ex. XIV: 4).

Both the Father and Zeus become angry with their recalcitrant followers. Though the rage of the classical deity is frequently stimulated by the behavior of the other gods (e.g., *Il*. VIII, 5–27), the Father's rage is stimulated by the war in heaven and exemplified in the Chariot of Paternal Deity, as it was in the *Iliad*, and by the passage of Sin and Death to the world already noted:

> My Hell-hounds, to lick up the draff and filth
> Which man's polluting Sin with taint hath shed
> On what was pure, till cramm'd and gorg'd, nigh burst
> With suckt and glutted offal, at one sling
> Of thy victorious Arm, well-pleasing Son,
> Both *Sin* and *Death*, and yawning *Grave* at last
> Through *Chaos* hurl'd, obstruct the mouth of Hell
> For ever, and seal up his ravenous Jaws (X, 630–7).

The Father's power, like Zeus', is based upon force as well as righteousness; 'ingrate, he had of mee/ All he could have; I made him just and right' (III, 97–8), the Father says of man, and His anger is equal to His sense of justice.

If the Father has the thunder of Zeus on His left, he has the mercy of Christianity on His right. Anger is eventually second to mercy. After the Father's display of Olympian anger, the Son offers to take on Himself the anger of God:

> Behold mee then, mee for him, life for life
> I offer, on mee let thine anger fall;
> . . . . .
> Then with the multitude of my redeem'd
> Shall enter Heav'n long absent, and return,
> Father, to see thy face, wherein no cloud
> Of anger shall remain, but peace assur'd,
> And reconcilement; wrath shall be no more (III, 236–7; 260–4).

It would not be far-fetched to see in this transition from anger to mercy, the shift from paganism to Christianity: the anger of Zeus is followed by the self-sacrifice of the Son. At the same time the Son accomplishes what the classical intercessors on behalf of man could never do: save him from death. Even Zeus' helplessness lies behind this scene, Zeus who could not save his own son at Troy. Like the Father, Zeus has more sympathy for man than for the rebellious deities, but he is powerless to save him because the Greek god has the power of destruction but not the power of salvation. The Father equals Zeus in his ability to harden hearts, but he excells him by having the power to soften hearts as well, as He does for Adam and Eve: 'Thus they in lowliest plight repentant stood/ Praying, for from the Mercy-seat above/ Prevenient Grace descending had remov'd/ The stony from thir hearts' (XI, 1–4). Often Zeus refuses prayers, as in the typical passage where Agamemnon prays for the death of Hector and the poet adds: '"Ως *ἔφατ', οὐδ' ἄρα πώ οἱ ἐπεκραίαινε Κρονίων,/ ἀλλ'ὅ γε δέκτο μὲν ἱρά, πόνον δ' ἀμέγαρτον ὄφελλεν*' (*Il.* II, 419–20; 'Thus he spoke, but the son of Kronos would by no means bring these things to pass, but received the sacrifices and increased dreadful suffering'). Similarly, Zeus refuses Achilles' prayer that Patroklos be brought back safely from battle (XVI, 250–2).

What the classical tradition invoked by Milton shows is that the relationship between man and god has changed as well as continued from the earlier epics. The Greeks and the Romans feared but did not love their gods. Man and god seldom confer in the classical epics, and the father of the gods and man never, but Adam actually argues with God for a mate. The distancing of the relationship of God and man is the legacy of the fall and is exemplified in the classical epics, but in *Paradise Lost*, the pristine relationship between God and man is momentarily restored.

The justice and mercy of God are the principal defenses of the ways of God to man. The first rests upon the assumption that man has free will, a claim that the Father makes: 'I made him just and right,/ Sufficient to have stood, though free to fall' (III, 98–9). The background of the three classical epics helps prove man's free will, if we accept Milton's reading of them, and I think we can. In his prose, Milton claims that the *Iliad* and the *Odyssey* were proof for the free will of man that existed *'besides fate'* (*Prose*, II, 294). Further, Milton found in the *Aeneid* (I, 39–41) an example of divine justice (*Prose*, VI, 387), where the sins of one sinner require expiation by a whole race. In his reading of the classical epics, Milton emphasizes that these epics are all partially theodicies: latent in the epic tradition is a defense of God's ways to man.[18] The *Iliad* shows us a philosophically vague but poetically vivid picture of the relationship between god and man, between fate and free will, and between god and fate. A similar series of relationships inform the *Aeneid*, but it is to the *Odyssey* that we must turn in order to see the key passage that influenced Milton's conception of his God. The passage that Milton referred to in his prose and that Northrop Frye suggests in passing as a source for the speeches of the Father in Book III[19] gave the plaintive tone, the pure style, and the basis of defense for the God of *Paradise Lost*:

οἱ δὲ δὴ ἄλλοι
Ζηνὸς ἐνὶ μεγάροισιν Ὀλυμπίου ἁθρόοι ἦσαν.
τοῖσι δὲ μύθων ἦρχε πατὴρ ἀνδρῶν τε θεῶν τε·
μνήσατο γὰρ κατὰ θυμὸν ἀμύμονος Αἰγίσθοιο,
τόν ῥ' Ἀγαμεμνονίδης τηλεκλυτὸς ἔκταν' Ὀρέστης·
τοῦ ὅ γ' ἐπιμνησθεὶς ἔπε' ἀθανάτοισι μετηύδα·
''Ὢ πόποι, οἷον δή νυ θεοὺς βροτοὶ αἰτιόωνται.
ἐξ ἡμέων γάρ φασι κάκ' ἔμμεναι· οἱ δὲ καὶ αὐτοὶ
σφῇσιν ἀτασθαλίῃσιν ὑπὲρ μόρον ἄλγε' ἔχουσιν,
ὡς καὶ νῦν Αἴγισθος ὑπὲρ μόρον Ἀτρεΐδαο
γῆμ' ἄλοχον μνηστήν, τὸν δ' ἔκτανε νοστήσαντα,
εἰδὼς αἰπὺν ὄλεθρον· ἐπεὶ πρό οἱ εἴπομεν ἡμεῖς,
Ἑρμείαν πέμψαντες, ἐΰσκοπον ἀργειφόντην,
μήτ' αὐτὸν κτείνειν μήτε μνάασθαι ἄκοιτιν·
ἐκ γὰρ Ὀρέσταο τίσις ἔσσεται Ἀτρεΐδαο,
ὁππότ' ἂν ἡβήσῃ τε καὶ ἧς ἱμείρεται αἴης.
ὣς ἔφαθ' Ἑρμείας, ἀλλ' οὐ φρένας Αἰγίσθοιο
πεῖθ' ἀγαθὰ φρονέων· νῦν δ' ἀθρόα πάντ' ἀπέτισε' (I, 26–43).

> (The other gods were together in the halls of Olympian Zeus, and the father of gods and men began to speak to them, for he remembered in his heart splendid Aigisthos, whom the far-famed son of Agamemnon, Orestes, killed. Remembering him, he spoke to the immortal gods: 'Alas, how men now find fault with the gods. They say evil comes from us, but they themselves have suffering due to their wicked deeds besides fate; as now besides his fate, Aigisthos married the wife of the son of Atreus and killed him returning home, Aigisthos knowing full well of [his own] utter destruction, since sending Hermes, sharp-sighted Argeiphontes, we told him before not to kill him nor to woo his wife. "For revenge will come from Orestes for the son of Atreus, when he comes of age and wants his land." Thus Hermes spoke, but these good intentions did not persuade the heart of Aigisthos; now he has atoned for all.')

This speech is the *locus classicus* of classical theodicy in epic poetry. Readers who remember this speech are likely to see in the Father's defensiveness a classical precedent:

> So will fall
> Hee and his faithless Progeny: whose fault?
> Whose but his own? ingrate, he had of mee
> All he could have; I made him just and right,
> Sufficient to have stood, though free to fall (III, 95–9).

Readers are also likely to recollect that Hermes corresponds to Raphael and Abdiel, the two divine warners, who warn man and the rebellious angels, respectively, of their false steps. As Milton reminds us by using this parallel, the *Odyssey* is an epic of trial and fall: the suitors, the crew of Odysseus, Melanthios, and the twelve maidservants are all tested, judged guilty, and destroyed; on the other hand, Penelope, Telemachos, Laertes, Eumaeus, and Phemios are tested, judged innocent, and saved. The action of the poem proves the justice claimed by Zeus in the opening speech, just as the action of *Paradise Lost* makes good the Father's claim for the free will of His creatures. Homer, Milton implies, had valid theological insights; he had caught a glimpse of God. He noticed God's concern for man, which Athene, like the Son brings up in response to the speech of the godhead, though her concern is only with Odysseus, while the Son is concerned with the whole human race.

Milton's God goes beyond Zeus, of course. He has endowed man with reason, so that He need not rely upon force alone, and

His greater power enables Him to do what Zeus often wanted to do but could not: save man's life. The Son's offer of His life for man's has no classical parallel and so it stands out all the more. Milton could have gone outside the epic tradition and have used Alcestis, as he did in his twenty-third sonnet, but the effect of the dropping of the epic background further away from the main action – it is never missing entirely – emphasizes the synthesis of Christianity with the epic tradition.

Milton has also turned the epic around. In the classical epic, man is so much the measure of all things that when Odysseus was offered immortality by Calypso, he refused it (*Od*. V, 203–24). The gods of Homer and Virgil do not live the vital lives of men; the classical epic centered itself, as Greek culture did, on man. Milton reverses this tradition and has put God back in the center of the epic world, although he works within the framework of the classical epic and uses more than he rejects. The Father emerges out of a cloud of classical error and is seen to be the true source of all virtue. Homer and Virgil were not wrong – Homer saw the faults of Achilles as well as anyone – but they did not see far enough into the theological workings of the world. Revealed truth shows that heaven is not at variance with classical art: angels, the Son, and the Father may have classical analogues within the confines of faith and reason.

3 'Et in Arcadia Ego': the conflict in Eden

While Satan is a perversion of classical epic values and the Father and the Son are a Christianization of those values, Adam and Eve must choose between the two. They begin in the purer state and fall into the sinful classicism of Satan and later partially regain their former purity. Again what is most important is the relevance of the classical epic to the developments in the poem, an aspect of *Paradise Lost* that has received little attention in regard to Eden, although Homer and Virgil have unwittingly contributed to Milton's earthly paradise.

If *Paradise Lost* has a hero in the classical sense of that term, he must be Adam. That Milton's hero has potential faults does not matter, for Odysseus, Aeneas, and especially Achilles were imperfect. That Milton's hero fails in his task does matter of course, for it changes the epic into tragedy. Adam's failure is quite different, however, from what might have occurred in the other epics had their heroes failed, for Adam's task is different. It is not martial success, which is transferred to the Son and others who fight for the godhead, but obedience to God. Adam loses the struggle because he chooses Eve over God and is thereby indirectly defeated by Satan. Yet this Christian story of temptation, fall, and partial redemption is told in classical terms: Adam – and, as we shall see later, Eve too – is built out of the classical epic; even their failure has epic precedent.

Adam has specific affinities with all the major classical epic heroes, besides sharing with them the general heroic qualities of eloquence, reason, beauty, strength, intellectual acumen, and sex appeal. His resemblance to Aeneas in the scene where Raphael resembles Mercury has already been discussed, so let us turn to his relationship to Achilles. Like Adam, Achilles is a deathbringer, as Homer tells us at the beginning of the *Iliad*:

Μῆνιν ἄειδε, θεά, Πηληϊάδεω 'Αχιλῆος
οὐλομένην, ἣ μυρί' 'Αχαιοῖς ἄλγε' ἔθηκε,
πολλὰς δ' ἰφθίμους ψυχὰς ''Αϊδι προΐαψεν

> ἡρώων, αὐτοὺς δὲ ἑλώρια τεῦχε κύνεσσιν
> οἰωνοῖσί τε πᾶσι, . . . (I, 1–5).
>
> (Sing, goddess, the destructive wrath of Peleus' son, Achilles, which brought much suffering to the Achaians and sent many glorious souls of heroes to Hades and made them prey to dogs and all kinds of birds, . . .)

Likewise Milton begins with the destruction brought by his hero: 'Of Man's First Disobedience, and the Fruit/ Of that Forbidden Tree, whose mortal taste/ Brought Death into the World, and all our woe' (I, 1–3). Homer in his invocation, we are reminded, did not emphasize the humanity of Achilles' handing over the body of Hector to Priam or his reconciliation with the heroic world but his destructiveness, and Milton has followed Homer in emphasizing the tragedy resulting from the story he is about to relate. Milton's poem is about the destruction of paradise and about the death of all men, as Homer's is about the destruction that resulted from the wrath of Achilles. The reference to the *Iliad* shows that Milton and Homer saw similar results from heroic hybris.

Milton also provides Adam with an Odyssean background. As a model of Christian behavior, Odysseus, as Milton noticed, is very adaptable to the ethics of Christianity since he has the patience and the endurance, the passive side of the classical hero, which comes closest to Christ Himself. If Satan represented a degenerate Odysseus, Adam represents a perfected one and an antithesis to Satan's Odyssean phase, as the Son was the antithesis to his Achillean phase. Milton alludes to the likeness between Eden and the garden of Alcinoös (V, 341); to that must be added Adam's 'Hyacinthine Locks' (IV, 301) which he shares with Odysseus (*Od*. VI, 231) and which is commonly annotated. As others have also noticed,[1] Adam does not appear until the fourth book, like Odysseus who does not appear until the fifth.

Though we must be careful in over-ascribing classical qualities to Adam, since many of the echoes before the fall are faint, the tradition behind the poem and the motifs that Milton has set up earlier often lead to Odysseus. Like Odysseus', Adam's strength lies in his reason, the power which enables both heroes to be admired by gods and which enables both heroes to interpret the dreams of their wives: Odysseus interprets Penelope's dream (*Od*. XIX, 555–8) and Adam interprets Eve's (V, 96–121). Disguised before Penelope, Odysseus predicts that the suitors will be killed, like the geese in the dream, and that the eagle who kills them is Odysseus, to which Penelope replies with the famous description of gates of horn which produce true dreams and of the gates of ivory which produce false dreams. Milton's scene is a redaction of this one, but the traditional description of the two gates (imitated in *Aen.* VI, 893–6) is dismissed in Adam's treatment, since man is no longer subject to the malicious whims of evil spirits:

> Evil into the mind of God or Man
> May come and go, so unapprov'd, and leave
> No spot or blame behind: Which gives me hope
> That what in sleep thou didst abhor to dream,
> Waking thou never wilt consent to do (V, 117–21).

Adam reasons out the cause of the dream, 'Some such resemblances methinks I find/ Of our last Ev'ning's talk, in this thy dream' (114–15). Like Odysseus', Adam's heroism rests upon his reason, the true Christian heroism that Milton found in Lactantius and adapted for his *Commonplace Book*: 'A man's courage depends, not upon his body, but upon his reason, which is man's strongest protection and defense' (*Prose*, I, 373). Adam reflects this power and echoes Odysseus' heroism of thought. He also resembles Odysseus in eloquence, a virtue lauded by Raphael: 'Nor are thy lips ungraceful, Sire of men,/ Nor tongue ineloquent; for God on thee/ Abundantly his gifts hath also pour'd' (VIII, 218–20). But Adam also shares a potential vice with Odysseus: Odysseus' fatal curiosity which dooms his men both in the land of the Laistrygonians and in the land of the Cyclops. Adam's curiosity is less physical than Odysseus' but none the less dangerous; Raphael asks him to control this faculty when he answers Adam's question about celestial motions:

> Heav'n is for thee too high
> To know what passes there; be lowly wise:
> Think only what concerns thee and thy being;
> Dream not of other Worlds, what Creatures there
> Live, in what state, condition or degree,
> Contented that thus far hath been reveal'd
> Not of Earth only but of highest Heav'n (VIII, 172–8).

If Adam's curiosity extends further than Odysseus', so does the humility with which he accepts such a rebuke: these words would be incomprehensible to Homer's hero.

Like Adam, Eve too has a classical stature, which again like

Adam's is developed through *contaminatio*. The standard analogues put forth have been Dido and Circe,[2] but I think we can go further, since here Milton uses the mythological embellishment common to the classical epic and a series of direct allusions which elevates Eve above her classical epic predecessors and foreshadows her fall. The beasts of the field are 'more duteous at her call,/ Than at *Circean* call the Herd disguis'd' (IX, 521–2), an allusion that puts her above Circe but also looks forward to her denigration of Adam through lust, 'As with new Wine intoxicated' (IX, 1008) they both fall to the Circean sty, another ethical similarity between Milton and Homer. Milton also employs a standard Renaissance mythological parallel: the resemblance between Pandora and Eve:

> And heav'nly Choirs the Hymenaean sung,
> What day the genial Angel to our Sire
> Brought her in naked beauty more adorn'd,
> More lovely than *Pandora* whom the Gods
> Endow'd with all their gifts (IV, 711–15).

Pandora's destructiveness is later replaced with that of the beauty contest on Mount Ida that eventually brought about the fall of Troy:

> *Eve*
> Undeckt, save with herself more lovely fair
> Than Wood-Nymph, or the fairest Goddess feign'd
> Of three that in Mount *Ida* naked strove (V, 379–82).

Though we see here a foreshadowing of the fall of Eden in the fall of Troy, it is the elevation of Eve that is most important in this prelapsarian picture of her:

> Thus saying, from her Husband's hand her hand
> Soft she withdrew, and like a Wood-Nymph light,
> *Oread* or *Dryad*, or of *Delia's* Train,
> Betook her to the Groves, but *Delia's* self
> In gait surpass'd (IX, 385–9).

Like the Son, Eve rises beyond epic and classical parallels. If she resembles Penelope in her discussion of dreams with Adam, she surpasses her in being present when Satan creates the first deluding dream for mankind; indeed she surpasses all the heroines of epic poetry. In spite of all that has been alleged against Milton's treatment of women[3] and in spite of the seventeenth-century conception of domestic hierarchy, Milton elevated Eve to full stature as an epic hero. Her part in the heroic action of *Paradise Lost* is central: she fights an epic battle as central as her male counterpart does, and she shares the consequences in full. Beside Eve, Penelope and Dido, moving as they are, are minor characters. Milton's internalizing of the concept of heroism to a moral struggle has opened the door for female heroism to enter fully armed into the epic tradition: it is Eve's strength combined with her capacity for love that later saves Adam. It remains one of Milton's contributions to the epic tradition that he made Eve part of the central action and changed the role of women in epic poetry.

The subtle linking of her to the epic tradition is not the least part of Milton's art. For instance, Eve is associated with flowers in the poem, symbols of her innocence and frailty, as when she leaves Adam in order:

> to support
> Each Flow'r of slender stalk, whose head though gay
> Carnation, Purple, Azure, or speckt with Gold,
> Hung drooping unsustain'd, them she upstays
> Gently with Myrtle band (IX, 427–31).

This tender image has already been overshadowed by an earlier one which associated the flowers of paradise with the fall of Proserpina, the classical Eve: the Garden of Eden is fairer than the place where '*Proserpin* gath'ring flow'rs/ Herself a fairer Flow'r by gloomy *Dis*/ Was gather'd' (IV, 269–71). Sometimes she is directly compared to a flower: 'Herself, though fairest unsupported Flow'r,/ From her best prop so far' (IX, 432–3). The sense of doom that Milton associates with the floral image of Eve culminates in the fall which takes place on a 'Flow'ry Plat' (IX, 456) and causes Adam to drop the garland of flowers that he had woven for Eve:

> *Adam* the while
> Waiting desirous of her return, had wove
> Of choicest Flow'rs a Garland to adorn
> Her Tresses, and her rural labors crown,
> . . . . .
> *Adam*, soon as he heard
> The fatal Trespass done by *Eve*, amaz'd,
> Astonied stood and Blank, while horror chill
> Ran through his veins, and all his joints relax'd;
> From his slack hand the Garland wreath'd for *Eve*
> Down dropp'd and all the faded Roses shed (IX, 838–41; 888–93)

Adam's later epithet for Eve 'deflow'r'd' (IX, 901) thus gains metaphorical weight.

The image is a natural outgrowth of the connection between Eden as a place and as a state of innocence from which Eve falls, an image that has a variety of sources, but is of particular relevance to the epic tradition.[4] There the fallen flower represents, among other things, a fallen warrior, a tradition that begins with Homer who tells us how Teukros, aiming an arrow at Hector, strikes Gorgythion who falls:

μήκων δ' ὡς ἑτέρωσε κάρη βάλεν, ἥ τ' ἐνὶ κήπῳ,
καρπῷ βριθομένη νοτίῃσί τε εἰαρινῇσιν,
ὣς ἑτέρωσ' ἤμυσε κάρη πήληκι βαρυνθέν (VIII, 306–8).

(Like a poppy, he bent his head to one side, a garden poppy weighed down with fruit and spring rain, thus his head drooped down under the weight of his helmet.)

This famous simile was doubled and expanded by Virgil. He used it for Pallas who was killed by Turnus:

qualem uirgineo demessum pollice florem
seu mollis uiolae seu languentis hyacinthi,
cui neque fulgor adhuc nec dum sua forma recessit,
non iam mater alit tellus uirisque ministrat (XI, 68–71).

(Like a flower plucked by a virgin finger, either of the soft violet or the drooping hyacinth, while neither its sheen nor its beauty has yet faded, but its mother the earth no longer nourishes it nor supplies its strength.)

And he used it for the dead Euryalus:

purpureus ueluti cum flos succisus aratro
languescit moriens, lassoue papauera collo
demisere caput pluuia cum forte grauantur (IX, 435–7).

(As when a purple flower cut down by a plow languishes dying or as poppies have drooped their heads upon their weary necks when weighed down by a chance shower.)

If Virgil expands and multiplies in order to emulate Homer, Milton's image of the fallen flower spreads throughout the poem and associates Eve with the fallen heroes of the classical epic. In Virgil, it is a beloved companion that has fallen, an idea we will see shifted to Eve from Patroklos in the argument with Adam. But the image in Milton is carried to its Christian conclusion: no longer is human life just a frail flower that may be violently cut down and wasted, but it also possesses the power of its own spiritualization as Raphael tells Adam:

> So from the root
> Springs lighter the green stalk, from thence the leaves
> More aery, last the bright consummate flow'r
> Spirits odorous breathes (V, 479–82).

The flower, like everything else in the epic tradition, leads, in *Paradise Lost*, to God.

On the other hand, Eve's elevation brings about the central conflict in the poem, a conflict that also grows out of the epic tradition. It is this conflict that begins the degeneration of Adam and Eve from the purified heroism of heaven to the degenerate heroism of Satan. For this change, Milton drew upon the traditional struggle between love and epic adventure and fixed it in the climactic center of *Paradise Lost*. Possibly Milton was following upon Tasso's justification of love as a theme even more worthy than war for epic treatment.[5] Undoubtedly he was following the epic tradition: in the *Iliad*, Hector must either remain with his pleading family or go out to fight Achilles; Odysseus must either stay with Calypso – or later Circe – or return to Ithaka; and Aeneas must either remain with Dido in Carthage or leave to found Rome. In *Paradise Lost*, Adam must choose between love for Eve and obedience to God. Eve too makes a choice between love and heroism but only after she falls. Her first choice is between vanity, self-love, and obedience, when she leaves Adam; later she chooses between accepting the consequences of eating the forbidden fruit and virtually killing Adam out of jealousy. It is her second choice that is a question of love and honor in the classical epic sense. In each epic there is a choice between love and the heroic action appropriate to that poem, and in each epic the classical heroes choose the heroic alternative over the affectionate, but in *Paradise Lost*, both heroes fail by choosing love over virtue.

Then they both fall into the corrupt classicism of Satan. Although Adam knows that Eve may be tempted if she is let tend the garden alone, he finally yields to her bruised feelings and lets her go. Thus he reverses the true heroic choice, and Adam becomes, like Satan, a corrupted hero. On the other hand it is Eve who chooses the Iliadic alternative: she hopes to confront and conquer the epic villain: 'his foul esteem/ Sticks no dishonor on our Front, but turns/ Foul on himself; then wherefore shunn'd or fear'd/ By us?' (IX, 329–32). Although Eve's heroism derives from the classical epic, her choice is wrong here; her true heroic task is the preservation of her virtue, as is Adam's. Each epic presents its own particular alternative: it would be equally absurd for Aeneas to return home, for Odysseus to found another city, or for Hector to leave Troy. Eve should have taken the precautions necessary to avoid temptation and fall if we judge her by the heroic choice offered in the poem, and Adam should have bid her stay. The epic tradition has not been abandoned here nor have the heroes become less active or more passive: Hector, Odysseus, and Aeneas all have to submit their wills to the fated word of god if they are to survive. Once the wrong decision is made the epic changes into tragedy. Tragedy may occur in any case, as with Dido, but Aeneas hardly has any choice given the world he inhabits, for his departure is ordered by Jupiter through Mercury. In the epics of Homer, Virgil, and Milton, love, in the human sense of that term, must not interfere with valor.

The degeneration of Adam and Eve is, as I said earlier, a fall from epic to tragedy. Such use of tragedy in an epic had theoretical and practical precedent. As Aristotle pointed out, epics contained material for tragedy,[6] and it was obvious to Milton where to look for epic examples. For a classicist like Milton the most obvious parallel to the separation of Adam and Eve, a separation that brings on the tragedy, was that of Dido and Aeneas, but Milton did not evoke that scene with any directness of allusion nor did he recast the departure of Odysseus from Aiaia or the arguments used to detain Hector from battle. Milton used another scene from classical epic for the *retractatio* of the separation of Adam and Eve, a scene in which Homer showed, not the workings of fate, but the free will that Milton lauded the Greek poet for recognizing: the separation of Patroklos and Achilles in *Iliad* XVI, a parallel that we may be grateful to Martin Mueller for noticing.[7]

The ideal of friendship that we find in the epic poems, in such relationships as Achilles and Patroklos and Aeneas and Achates, is perverted by Satan into the relationship between master and henchman that forms the basis for his friendship with Beelzebub; in fact Satan knows that he is damning his own friend along with all the rest of his followers. At the other end of the moral scale, we find the ideal of friendship transformed in heaven into the abstract love between the Father and the Son, a spiritualization of the friendship ideal of the *Odyssey* where the *comitas* ideal is shifted to the relationship between father and son and husband and wife. Milton further expanded the possibilities of epic friendship existing between man and woman that begin in the *Odyssey*.

But he based the separation of the two friends upon the separation of Patroklos and Achilles. Structurally both scenes occur at about the same place in each epic, two-thirds of the way through, and they consist in an argument about separation, the fall of the one who separates, and later the catastrophe which results from the argument, the death of the hero. It is the patterning of the two scenes that creates the parallel. Both arguments begin with the weaker of the two friends, Patroklos and Eve, asking to go forth alone. Patroklos wishes to repulse the Greeks in the guise of Achilles, and Eve hopes that she has the opportunity to repulse Satan, from which encounter she will 'double honor gain' (IX, 332). Eve thus shares already one of the pagan incentives to battle. Both aspirants are warned by their stronger friends of an enemy who will prove too strong for them: Patroklos knows that Hector must be avoided, but cannot resist taking him on when he meets with success on the field, while Eve immediately contemplates the glory that she will derive from repulsing Satan. When Adam relents, the narrator bursts in, forecasting her fall:

> O Much deceiv'd, much failing, hapless *Eve*,
> Of thy presum'd return! event perverse!
> Thou never from that hour in Paradise
> Found'st either sweet repast, or sound repose (IX, 404–7).

Similar foreshadowing occurs in Homer's scene:

> *Ὣς φάτο λισσόμενος μέγα νήπιος· ἦ γὰρ ἔμελλεν*
> *οἷ αὐτῷ θάνατόν τε κακὸν καὶ κῆρα λιτέσθαι* (XVI, 46–7).
>
> (Thus he spoke asking great things foolishly, for indeed it was as if he were asking for his own death and evil fate.)

As Mueller observes,[8] the narrator's burst of direct address, so rare in Homer and unique in Milton, is reserved for Eve, just as it is used for Patroklos: *'ἔνθ' ἄρα τοι, Πάτροκλε, φάνη βιότοιο τελευτή'* (XVI, 787; 'there the end of your life, Patroklos, was shown forth'). The downfall of the companion in both cases brings about the downfall of the hero too: Patroklos' death arouses Achilles to avenge him by killing Hector, Patroklos' slayer, with the full knowledge that Hector's death will lead to his own, just as Adam eats of the fruit, knowing full well that death will be the result. In this respect: Patroklos and Achilles act freely, a fact which helps to remind us that Adam and Eve do also.

The echo also begins the degeneration of Adam and Eve into the type of perverted classical figures that Satan represented. For instance, we saw that Adam possessed an innocent curiosity that contrasted with Satan's destructive curiosity and was a faint echo of Odysseus. As we approach the fall, Eve's tone becomes more hybristic and self-glorifying: she is susceptible already to Satan's pagan temptations, though her will remains free.

Eve finds Satan in the same way that Nausicaa finds the wily Odysseus, amid the bower of paradise, but with very different results. The Adversary praises her as a goddess for her 'Celestial Beauty' (IX, 540) and suggests her apotheosis: she is one 'who shouldst be seen/ A Goddess among Gods' (546–7). These words call to mind the words of Odysseus to Nausicaa: *'Γουνοῦμαί σε, ἄνασσα· θεός νύ τις ἦ βροτός ἐσσι'* (*Od*. VI, 149, 'Mistress, I ask you, are you divine or human?'). It is not unusual that the two archetypal deceivers would resort to the same what's-a-nice-girl-like-you-doing-in-a-place-like-this approach, since neither Nausicaa nor Eve is familiar with it.

That Eve is confronting the embodiment of her future degeneration into the classical vice is evident in the ill-omened raiment of Satan. In order to see this warning in the transformation of Satan into the serpent, we must recall that in the classical epic the serpent is a bad omen (*Il*. II, 308–9; XI, 39–40; *Aen*. VII, 346–53). The *locus classicus* that Milton's serpent invokes is Virgil's description of the two serpents that crush Laocoön and his children and prepare the way for the destruction of Troy, just as Satan as serpent prepares the way for the destruction of Eden. The two passages are so unique in epic poetry that there can be little doubt that Milton is emulating Virgil, as Virgil frequently emulated Homer, yet this source has been strangely neglected.[9] Virgil's passage reads:

> ecce autem gemini a Tenedo tranquilla per alta
> (horresco referens) immensis orbibus angues
> incumbunt pelago pariterque ad litora tendunt;
> pectora quorum inter fluctus arrecta iubaeque
> sanguineae superant undas, pars cetera pontum
> pone legit sinuatque immensa uolumine terga (II, 203–8).

> (But behold from Tenedos over the calm ocean (I shrink from telling it) twin serpents with huge coils lean over the sea and together race for the shore, their breasts are erect amidst the

> sea and their blood-red crests tower above the waves. The rest of them behind passes over the sea and twists their huge backs in many a fold.)

Milton's rival passage reads:

> toward *Eve*
> Address'd his way, not with indented wave,
> Prone on the ground, as since, but on his rear,
> Circular base of rising folds, that tow'r'd
> Fold above fold a surging Maze, his Head
> Crested aloft, and Carbuncle his Eyes;
> With burnisht Neck of verdant Gold, erect
> Amidst his circling Spires, that on the grass
> Floated redundant (IX, 495–503).

Milton suggests Virgil's serpent by the coils (Milton's 'Spires'), the upright position, and the horrible beauty of Satan's form, though without the epic tradition constantly alluded to in *Paradise Lost*, these clues would hardly be enough. But the metaphor of the serpent's progress through water ('surging Maze,' 'floated redundant') brings Virgil to mind immediately, therefore re-enforcing the parallel between the destruction of Troy and the destruction of Eden. The second event has now displaced the former as the central event in epic poetry just as the fall had displaced the Trojan War as the most cataclysmic event in human history and Eve, though responsible for her fate, takes the place of Laocoön, which arouses some sympathy for her, while Satan's appearance signals her degeneration.

Eve is also the Helen of Milton's story, a heroine whose fall destroys the world around her. Satan's temptation is in many ways a temptation to adopt a degenerate pagan view of the world. In order to persuade her, Satan employs the oratory of '*Athens* and free *Rome*,' a fitting style for a plea to arouse a goddess's sense of epic heroism. Satan asks Eve to set herself up as a hero who defies death and accomplishes great things on her own, things which even God will praise:

> will God incense his ire
> For such a petty Trespass, and not praise
> Rather your dauntless virtue, whom the pain
> Of Death denounc't, whatever thing Death be (IX, 692–5).

Satan tempts Eve to make the fatal mistake of classical theology, to assume that God is like man, although no classical hero would ever presume to become a god and, as we noticed before, no true classical hero is ever irreverent. Satan's presumption is more characteristic of tragic 'hybris' than epic egotism. To his own tragic, rather than epic state, he invites Eve:

> What can your knowledge hurt him, or this Tree
> Impart against his will if all be his?
> Or is it envy, and can envy dwell
> In heav'nly breasts? (IX, 727–30).

As is often footnoted, the last question echoes Virgil's question at the opening of the *Aeneid*: 'tantaene animis celestibus irae? (*Aen.* I, 11; 'is there so much wrath in heavenly hearts?'). The main point of the argument is that Eve can be a god, since, as Satan implies, there is a plurality of gods: 'ye shall be as Gods' (IX, 708).[10]

Substituting pagan 'hybris' for Christian obedience, Eve eats the apple of discord and becomes a devotee of animism who worships the tree: 'O Sovran, virtuous, precious of all Trees/ In Paradise, of operation blest/ To Sapience' (IX, 795–7). That Eve is becoming a superstitious pagan is suggested by the narrator himself:

> So saying, from the Tree her step she turn'd,
> But first low Reverence done, as to the power
> That dwelt within, whose presence had infus'd
> Into the plant sciential sap, deriv'd
> From Nectar, drink of Gods (IX, 834–8).

Raphael drinks wine, we remember; it was a Homeric error that the 'Gods' drank nectar. In other words, Eve has adopted the superstitions of the classical world, since these superstitions flatter her selfish desires. It is the world of Virgil's Polydorus, now a tree spirit, and of Virgil's golden bough, the key to the underworld, that Eve now enters.

By classicizing this incident Milton suggests that Homer and Virgil had intimations of the fall. The theme of food forbidden by a deity runs through the classical epic in the sacred cattle of the Sun in the *Odyssey* (XII, 260–419) and in the sacred cattle of the Harpies in the *Aeneid* (III, 219–69). These incidents are vestiges of the fall found in classical epic, further indications to Milton of the free will of man that he found in Homer and Virgil. Like these classical transgressors, Eve falls, making a synthesis of the classical and biblical traditions.

Eve also joins in another classical motif: she becomes like the classical heroes a deathbringer; Achilles, Odysseus, and Aeneas are all in their ways bringers of death, but Eve brings more: she brings about the death of the whole race of men, brings even the thing itself first into the world, so that the inscription that Poussin placed upon the tombstone in his paradise *'Et in Arcadia Ego'*[11] where the 'I' is death might serve as the epitaph for Milton's Eden. For a while Eve is the only deathbringer in *Paradise Lost*, an office that signifies her ironic elevation to the status of fallen hero.

Eve falls into other vices found in the classical world and exemplified by Satan. We saw her degenerate into the pagan worship of the tree after her fall; after that she begins to plot the downfall of Adam:

> what if God have seen,
> And Death ensue? then I shall be no more,
> And *Adam* wedded to another *Eve*,
> Shall live with her enjoying, I extinct;
> A death to think. Confirm'd then I resolve,
> *Adam* shall share with me in bliss or woe (IX, 826–31).

She then takes on Satan's role as a degenerate Odyssean deceiver, relying on false rhetoric and inspired by 'hybris.' When she first speaks to Adam in her 'alter'd style,' she asks: 'What words have past thy Lips' (IX, 1132; 1144), thereby echoing the familiar Homeric formula for annoyance or anger, a loss of rational control: *'ποῖόν σε ἔπος φύγεν ἕρκος ὀδόντων;'* ('What word escaped from your lips' (literally 'the barrier of your teeth')).[12] An even stronger echo resounds when nature reacts to Eve's tasting of the fruit: 'Earth felt the wound, and Nature from her seat/ Sighing through all her Works gave signs of woe,/ That all was lost' (IX, 782–4). As Addison noticed,[13] Milton is echoing the fall of Dido:

> prima et Tellus et pronuba Iuno
> dant signum; fulsere ignes et conscius aether
> conubiis summoque ulularunt uertice Nymphae.
> ille dies primus leti primusque malorum
> causa fuit; neque enim specie famaue mouetur
> nec iam furtiuum Dido meditatur amorem:
> coniugium uocat, hoc praetexit nomine culpam (IV, 166–72).

> (Both primal earth and Juno, Goddess of marriage, give the sign: fires flashed and the heavens shone, witness to their marriage, and the nymphs cried out on the mountain top. That day was the first day of destruction and the first cause of evil, for Dido is unmoved by appearance or reputation nor

> does she consider her love secret any longer. She calls it marriage and covers over sin with that name.)

Milton's passage extends the significance of the earlier one: we are reminded that Dido's fall suggests only the Punic Wars between Rome and Carthage, not the birth of evil itself, while Milton insists that Eve's fall is more important than Dido's and that Eve displaces Dido as the major tragic heroine of epic poetry.

If the passage analyzed above 'corrects' Virgil, the scene where Adam and Eve make love after the fall corrects Homer:

> So said he, and forebore not glance or toy
> Of amorous intent, well understood
> Of *Eve*, whose Eye darted contagious Fire.
> Her hand he seiz'd, and to a shady bank,
> Thick overhead with verdant roof imbower'd
> He led her nothing loath; Flow'rs were the Couch,
> Pansies, and Violets, and Asphodel,
> And Hyacinth, Earth's freshest softest lap.
> There they thir fill of Love and Love's disport
> Took largely, of thir mutual guilt the Seal,
> The solace of thir sin, till dewy sleep
> Oppress'd them, wearied with thir amorous play (IX, 1034–45).

As is well known, this scene is a *retractatio* of the scene where Hera seduces Zeus on Mount Ida and the earth bursts into 'fresh lotus and crocus and hyacinth' (*Il.* XIV, 348). Homer's scene is probably one of those that Milton alluded to as being deemed one of the 'undecent things' that Homer wrote about the gods (*Prose*, I, 891). Milton has properly transferred Homer's inappropriate behavior to his human characters and thus corrects a theological nod in the Greek poet; such behavior fits better with a Paris and a Helen than with the immortals, just as Milton transfers the domestic bickering of Zeus and Hera to Adam and Eve for a similar reason. In a way Adam and Eve have displaced Paris and Helen as the most destructive lovers in epic poetry, a displacement that is aided by the above parallel, for Hera's purpose in seducing Zeus is to allow Poseidon and other gods time to destroy the Trojans. So Adam and Eve fall into lust while the whole world is being destroyed. The flowers that burgeon beneath each pair of lovers remind us of the indifference of these two pairs of lovers to the fate of men: of the indifference of Zeus to the fate of the Trojans and of the indifference of Adam and Eve to the fate of their offspring, the human race. Milton adds one important detail that shifts his view of the scene away from Homer's when, instead of the golden cloud of dew that falls upon Zeus and Hera in order to induce sleep, Adam and Eve are surrounded by noxious vapors that arise from the gastronomical complications of eating the forbidden fruit (IX, 1044–51). If the image is disgusting, that is the point. In the background is the frail flower of human life that we noticed earlier in Homer, Virgil, and Milton.

The destruction of Eden is presented in distinctly classical terms. First Milton alludes to the myths of Janus and Hermes in the descent of Michael (XI, 129–33); then the dawn of the last day begins 'Her rosy progress,' reminiscent of Homer. An eagle appears in the sky in the manner of a Homeric omen:

> The Bird of *Jove*, stoopt from his aery tow'r,
> Two Birds of gayest plume before him drove:
> Down from a Hill the Beast that reigns in Woods,
> First hunter then, pursu'd a gentle brace,
> Goodliest of all the Forest, Hart and Hind;
> Direct to th' Eastern Gate was bent thir flight (XI, 185–90).

The omen of the predatory eagle is used by Homer to forecast the destruction of the suitors in the *Odyssey* (II, 146–76), to warn the Trojans on the battlefield (XII, 200–7), and to accompany Hermes' descent at the end of the *Iliad* (XXIV, 314–21). In each of these cases the heroes must interpret the sign from Zeus as Satan had to interpret the scales in Eden. Now Adam tries and fails (XI, 193–207), as he and Eve begin to pass into the real classical era. What Adam cannot see is that the ferocious world of the Homeric simile and the world of corrupt classicism represented by Satan are beginning here.

In the aftermath of the fall, Adam, like Eve in the temptation scene, represents the fallen side of the classical hero. Like Eve, Adam too is a degeneration of certain aspects of the classical hero: if she was the death-bringer, he is now the hero who must confront his death with full awareness. This confrontation is a development out of the whole epic tradition: each of the major heroes knows that he is going to die and his reaction to this news is a kind of test. In the *Iliad*, Hector states his acceptance of the price of heroism (VI, 488–9) and Achilles knows that his death follows upon Hector's and so, when his horse Xanthos speaking through the power of Hera reminds him that his death is soon, Achilles gruffly accepts his fate and tells Xanthos that he will neither refrain from fighting nor spare Hector in order to save his own life (XIX, 404–24). In the *Odyssey*, Odysseus received a prophecy of his death from Teiresias in the underworld and gave an answer as brusque as Achilles': Odysseus simply and acerbically stating that he accepts it (*Od*. XI, 134–9). In the *Aeneid*, the hero does not confront the future directly, as in the other two epics, but Jupiter prophesies his death and elevation which will occur three years after the conquest of Latium (I, 257–66). Venus, who listens to the prophecy, does not, like Thetis, tell her son, but Anchises, who displaces Teiresias as the epic prophet, consoles Aeneas with the achievements of his descendants (VI, 756–800). In *Paradise Lost*, the hero not only must accept death but must accept himself as the cause of it, a connection that could make no sense in the world of pagan epic (except in the *Odyssey*), where death is simply the price of life and the will of fate. This pagan epic world became associated, as we saw earlier, with mortality itself which is a major theme of the three classical epics, if we view them together. In a sense, to fall in Milton's poem is to live in the world of pagan mortality.

After the fall, it is Adam especially who descends into the world of pagan epic thought and who must work his way through the degenerate classicism represented by hell to the purified classicism represented by heaven. At first, he becomes a fallen Aeneas, a hero who did not heed the warning of God's messenger and who fell into uxoriousness. So Adam falls below his classical counterparts: he is the only one of our major epic heroes who fails in his major task: to preserve himself free from the sin of disobedience and so defeat his adversary. He falls into the vices and errors of paganism. When he berates Eve for leading him into sin (one could hardly imagine such lamentations from Achilles, Odysseus, or Aeneas), he condemns her whole sex: 'this fair defect/ Of Nature' (X, 891–2) in the same way that Agamemnon, betrayed by Clytemnestra, condemns the whole sex, excepting only Penelope, and her, it seems, only because he is talking to Odysseus (*Od*. XI, 436–56). Both fallen heroes forget what Zeus says at the beginning of the *Odyssey* and God in Book III of *Paradise Lost*: man is more responsible than anything else for his own fate.

Adam becomes so pagan in his immediate post-lapsarian state that he reacts to Michael's message of expulsion with a piety worthy of Aeneas, but as out of place here as Eve's heroism in challenging Satan:

> So many grateful Altars I would rear
> Of grassy Turf, and pile up every Stone
> Of lustre from the brook, in memory,
> Or monument to Ages, and thereon
> Offer sweet smelling Gums and Fruits and Flow'rs (XI, 323–7).

After the fall, Adam dwells in the world of fate and despair that Satan created by his fall and which had its roots in classical soil. Adam's despair leads him to lament his creation: 'Wherefore didst thou beget me? I sought it not' (X, 762). A similar despair informs Andromache's lament for Hector wherein she wishes that her father 'had never begotten' her (*'ὡς μὴ ὤφελλε τεκέσθαι'*; XXII, 481). Adam's despair is the despair of the *Iliad* where Zeus says that of all earthly creatures man is the most wretched (XVII, 446–7), but no true epic hero would ever utter such a remark, especially out of self-pity.

Like many classical heroes, Adam must face mortality with little consolation and no afterlife. The many parallels already suggested between Troy and Eden – Eve as Atê (the bringer of the apple of discord), the allusions to the fatal beauty contest judged upon Mount Ida, the uxoriousness of Adam and Zeus, and the parallel between the love-making of Adam and Eve and of Zeus and Hera, besides the natural paralleling of the two most important events in epic poetry and other allusions – culminate in the destruction of Eden which resembles the fall of Troy in the *Aeneid*.[14]

For this sad task, Michael appears:

> Not in his shape Celestial, but as Man
> Clad to meet Man; over his lucid Arms
> A military Vest of purple flow'd
> Livelier than *Meliboean*, or the grain
> Of *Sarra*, worn by Kings and Heroes old
> In time of Truce (XI, 239–44).

His cloak is like Cloanthus' in Virgil, a cloak also made of 'Melibean' (Tyrian) purple (V, 251), which is the same woven for classical heroes; its colors are those of 'Iris'; a helmet is on his head; he wears a 'zodiac' with a sword hung from it; and he carries a spear: in short he looks like a great classical warrior, even, it is suggested, greater. The glory that is usually reserved for the epic hero is transferred to Michael, as we saw earlier it was transferred to Raphael, in contrast to the descriptions of Satan as unglamorous warrior. The *ekphrasis* pertaining to the classical world belongs to God's servant, and the task of destroying the damned city of man is no longer given to Greeks but to angels: it is through God's will that Eden will be destroyed, not through the working out of fate before the eyes of a helpless Zeus.

As a result of Michael's visit, when Adam and Eve, like Aeneas, begin their search for a new Troy, much has changed since the fall. They do not leave paradise as fallen classical heroes; they develop beyond them for they learn that they have free will, that divine love is redemption, and that God's grace extends to all. Achilles, Odysseus, and Aeneas learn that they can have little effect on their own mortality, never could consider love as a sacrifice in the way that Eve and the Son offer themselves for others, and never could imagine immortality, except with dismay: Achilles in the underworld tells us that he would do the meanest chores if he could only return to earth (*Od.* XI, 489–91). Milton has changed this attitude: this world is no longer the goal of epic heroes but the next.

The process that Adam and Eve endure in order to arrive at self-knowledge is not beyond the range of the classical epic: Achilles and Telemachos also go through a *paideia* from which they emerge as wiser heroes. Like Aeneas examining the prophecies of his new kingdom, Milton's heroes must also sift out the meaning of a prophecy: the seed of the woman shall 'bruise/ The Serpent's head' (X, 1031–2), the terror of the classical serpent will be quelled. Like Achilles (in the *Odyssey*), Odysseus, and Aeneas, Adam and Eve must consider their offspring though, unlike the classical heroes, they have some control over their welfare if they can repent. From the viewpoint of the epic tradition, what Adam and Eve gain in the last part of the poem is perspective on the classical world that they are about to enter, a perspective on the philosophy behind the epic poems. That perspective is provided by Michael.

Michael's purpose is to transform the degenerate classicism of Adam and Eve into a philosophy consistent with Christianity. It is Michael who welds Christian and pagan philosophy into a coherent system. For the reader, Michael provides a proper reading of the classical epic and its philosophies and provides the most coherent and direct synthesis that Milton could muster of the classical and Christian worlds. Michael is not only the grace and the vengeance of God; he is an elevated vision of the ancients, as his costume implies, and a partial reinstatement of

Adam and Eve into that pure state of classical and biblical purity that they have lost. If Michael casts down sleep upon Eve, as Athene casts down sleep upon Penelope (*Od.* XIX, 604–5), he sends her only true dreams and true prophecies, unlike those of Satan. He shows Adam the rainbow that follows the flood, a symbol of God's covenant with man (XI, 865), which biblical commentators did not hesitate to see reflected in the classical figure of Iris, the messenger of the gods, who is most conspicuous in the *Aeneid*.[15]

Michael's teaching aims at, among other things, the guidance of Adam through the pagan world into which he has now fallen and the guidance of the reader through epic poetry with a Christian reading of the classical texts. When Adam, like Agamemnon (*Od.* XI, 436–56), blames the whole female sex for the fall, Michael corrects them both:

> To whom thus *Adam* of short joy bereft.
> O pity and shame, that they who to live well
> Enter'd so fair, should turn aside to tread
> Paths indirect, or in the mid way faint!
> But still I see the tenor of Man's woe
> Holds on the same, from Woman to begin.
> From Man's effeminate slackness it begins,
> Said th' Angel, who should better hold his place
> By wisdom, and superior gifts receiv'd (XI, 628–36).

Michael echoes the words of God and Zeus: that man is responsible for his own fate. To Adam's impulse to build altars of turf and stone, Michael replies 'thou know'st Heav'n his, and all the Earth,/ Not this Rock only; his Omnipresence fills/ Land, Sea, and Air' (XI, 335–7). Unlike pagan theology, true Christian theology insists that 'God áttributes to place/ No sanctity' (XI, 836–7). The piety of Aeneas cannot be fully imitated by Christians.

Another correction of classical values that Michael offers is the substitution of humility for the egotistical side of epic heroism. There is, after all, a possibility that Adam in his depraved state could further follow the example of Satan as a degenerate classical hero, a possibility that is not remote since Adam is entering an age when 'Might only shall be admir'd/ And Valor and Heroic Virtue call'd' (XI, 689–90). The counter example to heroic 'hybris' is the behavior of the Hebrews who take to the desert:

> Lest ent'ring on the *Canaanite* alarm'd
> War terrify them inexpert, and fear

> Return them back to *Egypt*, choosing rather
> Inglorious life with servitude; for life
> To noble and ignoble is more sweet
> Untrain'd in Arms, where rashness leads not on (XII, 217–22).

Michael's words take us back to Moloch's bald statement of epic heroism: 'My sentence is for open War: Of Wiles/ More unexpert, I boast not' (II, 51–2). Michael's rejecting of epic heroism also has its echo in classical literature itself in a proverb that appears in Greek and Latin: *'γλυκὺ δ' ἀπείροισι πόλεμος'*; 'dulce bellum inexpertis' ('war is sweet to the inexperienced').[16] Thus Michael uses the classics in their proper perspective for tutoring Adam. Michael of course rejects the excess of heroism, 'rashness,' not the heroic spirit itself. Even martial valor has its place if needed by God.

Beside the classical epic egotism that Michael holds up as no longer viable, the archangel places the true heroes who imitate the Son. For a while these heroes will suffer at the hands of the others, their 'proudest persecutors' (XII, 497), in whose ranks we may include Cain, Nimrod, and Pharaoh, all Satanic epic heroes. As Hughes notes, Milton deliberately echoes the description of Achilles' shield in the *Iliad* (XVIII, 478–616) in Michael's elaborate picture of the embattled world of epic heroism that follows the fall. In order to feel its non-biblical flavor, it must be quoted in full:

> He look'd and saw wide Territory spread
> Before him, Towns, and rural works between,
> Cities of Men with lofty Gates and Tow'rs,
> Concourse in Arms, fierce Faces threat'ning War,
> Giants of mighty Bone, and bold emprise;
> Part wield thir Arms, part curb the foaming Steed,
> Single or in Array of Battle rang'd
> Both Horse and Foot, nor idly must'ring stood;
> One way a Band select from forage drives
> A herd of Beeves, fair Oxen and fair Kine
> From a fat Meadow ground; or fleecy Flock,
> Ewes and thir bleating Lambs over the Plain,
> Thir Booty; scarce with Life the Shepherds fly,
> But call in aid, which makes a bloody Fray;
> With cruel Tournament the Squadrons join;
> Where Cattle pastur'd late, now scatter'd lies
> With Carcasses and Arms th' ensanguin'd Field
> Deserted; Others to a City strong
> Lay Siege, encampt; by Battery, Scale, and Mine,

> Assaulting; others from the wall defend
> With Dart and Jav'lin, Stones and sulphurous Fire;
> On each hand slaughter and gigantic deeds.
> In other part the scepter'd Heralds call
> To Council in the City Gates: anon
> Grey-headed men and grave, with Warriors mixt,
> Assemble, and Harangues are heard, but soon
> In factious opposition, till at last
> Of middle Age one rising, eminent
> In wise deport, spake much of Right and Wrong,
> Of Justice, of Religion, Truth and Peace,
> And Judgment from above: him old and young
> Exploded, and had seiz'd with violent hands,
> Had not a Cloud descending snatch'd him thence
> Unseen amid the throng: so violence
> Proceeded, and Oppression, and Sword-Law
> Through all the Plain, and refuge none was found (XI, 638–73).

The story of Enoch referred to at the end of this vision does not contain any of these elements (cf. Gen. V: 21–4): they are mostly borrowed from Homer's shield of Achilles where there is the same world of war, cattle rustling, siege, heralds, councils, and sword-law – in short, it is a picture of a world almost always at strife. But in *Paradise Lost*, this vision is no longer presented upon a shield, as it is in Homer – Satan's shield we remember was 'spotty' – but is presented as a phase of history, a pagan interlude between the Christian beginning and the Christian end of the world. This interlude bursts into the world with the fall of paradise and is reflected in the incursions that the warriors make into the pastoral world in the vision, a theme which appears in Homer too but here is given a Christian interpretation. Enoch shows the passive new hero whom God prefers to his more violent counterpart, a hero who will not accomplish 'great exploits' while 'of true virtue void' (XI, 790), but

> by small
> Accomplishing great things, by things deem'd weak
> Subverting worldly strong, and worldly wise
> By simply meek; that suffering for Truth's sake
> Is fortitude to highest victory,
> And to the faithful Death the Gate of Life (XII, 566–71).

In this education of the hero, Michael deliberately takes over the roles of Teiresias and Anchises, the two other major prophets in classical epic. As in the scene with Raphael, Milton here chooses to follow closely the *Aeneid*. Both prophets present a view of history, the latter prophet echoing the former. One such parallel was noticed by Addison:[17] Michael says that, ' "Things by thir names I call, though yet unnam'd" ' (XII, 140) echoing Anchises 'haec tum nomina erunt, nunc sunt sine nomine terrae' (VI, 776; 'these will be their names then; now these lands have no names'). Both prophets paint history with blood and gloom, and both prophets tell of a future hero who will put an end to strife: Anchises tells of Augustus and Michael tells of Christ. The process is one of displacement and correction of Virgil's prophecy: the Son displaces Augustus as the true promised man. Augustus will be an aristocrat, but Jesus a man of the lowest classes, and as Milton suggested in 'On the Morning of Christ's Nativity,' it is the Son of God who really brings the *pax romana*, not Augustus (ll. 54–60). Anchises promises that Roman rule will ' "equalize heaven and earth" ' (' "imperium terris, animos aequabit Olympo" '; VI, 782), and the new king will bring back the age of gold:

> 'hic uir, hic est, tibi quem promitti saepius audis,
> Augustus Caesar, diui genus, aurea condet
> saecula qui rursus Latio regnata per arua
> Saturno quondam' (VI, 791–4).
>
> ('This is he, this is the man whom you often heard promised to you, Augustus Caesar, A God's son, who will reestablish the golden ages in Latium in fields once ruled by Saturn.')

Michael replaces Augustus with the Messiah who will reestablish harmony and be the true ruler of the world: 'he shall ascend/ The Throne hereditary, and bound his Reign/ With earth's wide bounds, his glory with the Heav'ns' (XII, 369–71), another often cited but unexplicated parallel.[18] The echo seems deliberate, the purpose of which is to stress the change from the Virgilian world picture.

The message to the hero has also changed. Anchises' exalted advice to Aeneas, advice which sums up the dual purpose of the empire, could not apply to Adam:

> 'Romane, memento
> (hae tibi erunt artes), pacique imponere morem,
> parcere subiectis et debellare superbos' (VI, 851–3).
>
> ('Roman, remember (these will be your arts) to impose

civilization on peace, to spare the cast-down, and to war against the arrogant.')

The political virtue of the Romans no longer suits the new hero nor does the Roman arrogance of ruling the world. In *Paradise Lost*, it is the Son who sets order on peace (by replacing the uprooted hills, VI, 781–4), spares the suppliant, and casts down the proud. Michael's message shows the bloodshed that resulted from Roman, even classical, arrogance on the battlefield. Adam is to cultivate an inner sanctity: 'only add/ Deeds to thy knowledge answerable, add Faith,/ Add Virtue, Patience, Temperance, add Love' (XII, 581–3) so that he shall 'possess/ A paradise within thee, happier far' (XII, 586–7). For this change of view, Milton lifted the epic prophecy out of the gloom of the underworld where we find it in Homer and Virgil and raised it up on the Mount where the Son rejected the temptations of Satan. Michael has also extended, baptized, and internalized the prophecy of Anchises.

But the classical world has not been destroyed, only extended and completed. The classical world that Adam and Eve and their descendants are about to enter is now put into a Christian perspective, just as the classical epic is put into Christian perspective for the reader. The classical analogues, unlike those at the beginning of the poem, are now in the background. The rainbow of the covenant is more of a biblical allusion than a reference to Iris, and the cloud that snatches Enoch (XI, 670) belongs more to God than to Aphrodite. The hero may now take up arms, but he no longer can claim glory for himself: all power comes from the Maker and should be directed at God's enemies: 'also arm/ With spiritual Armor, able to resist/ *Satan's* assaults' (XII, 490–2). The proper militant stand is represented in Michael's classical finery and his classical cohort (XI, 239–50; 127–33). When Eve awakes, she exclaims 'Whence thou return'st, and whither went'st, I know;/ For God is also in sleep, and Dreams advise' (XII, 610–11) and ascribes another classical motif to God. Some of the virtues listed by Michael are common enough in the classical world – 'Virtue, Patience, Temperance,' and love (XII, 583), which are virtues in the classical epic also. Adam is asked to avoid those desires that drove Satan and the classical heroes to act like gods and to adopt the humility of Christianity first, then to seek for classical wisdom. Both Adam and Eve are urged to be 'lowly wise' because the heroism of the classical world is such that only the Son can attain it and then only with the help of the Father. Since even Satan's power is beyond human achievement, the human classical hero too has been humbled. The departure of Adam and Eve still occasions epic similes:

High in Front advanc't,
The brandisht Sword of God before them blaz'd
Fierce as a Comet; which with torrid heat,
And vapor as the *Libyan* Air adust,
Began to parch that temperate Clime (XII, 632–6).

Epic similes once signalled the degenerate world of Satan, but now Adam and Eve, and the reader of classical epic as well, have the perspective of Christian revelation with which to endure or to examine, as the case may be, the classical world. As epic characters, Adam and Eve develop beyond the limit of the classical heroes, a development made possible by the grace of God. But it is through the classical epic that we can more fully understand them.

4 Equal in renown: structure, style, and epic voice

So far we have considered the three spatial units of Milton's epic and have found hell, heaven, and Eden to possess classical landscapes. The same must be said of the structure, style, and epic narrator: they too are partially adaptations of the work of Homer and Virgil for Milton's Christian purposes. As much has already been said about the style of *Paradise Lost*, I have least to add here, but little has been said on the structure and virtually nothing on the narrator in relation to the classical epic, so I shall try to provide new readings of these two aspects of *Paradise Lost*. I shall begin with the structure.

Milton has led the reader from the degenerate classicism of Satan, a biblical figure who became classicized, to the purified classicism of Michael, an Anchises who has become Christianized and who opens the heroic era of Greece and Rome for Adam and Eve. At the same time, the reader has been led from the epic conventions almost in their bald state, the descent and the council, to a synthesis of classical ideals that are not at variance with those of Christianity. We have been shunted from epic convention to biblical revelation without losing sight of the epic. For this transformation the poet needed a different structure from the classical epic: as we have already noticed, the descent is separated from the prophecy and placed at the opposite end of the poem, a device that emphasizes how far away hell is from truth. In other classical epics, the descent with its prophecy lies in the middle of the poem: Book XI in the *Odyssey* and Book VI in the *Aeneid*.

From the point of view of epic conventions, we may divide *Paradise Lost* into six parts, each of which may be found in the classical epics, although Milton has changed the space allotted to each of these conventions. Critics have usually seen in *Paradise Lost* a reflection of the structure of the *Aeneid*.[1] I propose a broader interpretation. Here we must keep in mind that all the scenes in Milton's poem are composed out of the conventions of the classical epic rather than the folktale method of the Bible, that is, his poem comprises councils, rhetorical speeches, flytings, scales, shifting of scene among earth, hell, and heaven, invocations to the muse, catalogues, allegorical interludes, games, descriptions of technical processes, descents, prophecies and prophetic dreams, a tale within the tale, an epic narrator, battles, and a journey through supernatural obstacles, rather than biblical devices, such as parables, proverbs, genealogies, evangelical passages, depictions of judges and kings, a concern for the chosen people, and an omniscient narrator.

Each of the six parts of the poem reworks one traditional epic convention, while within each is subsumed several other epic conventions, the emphasis given to each convention illustrating a Miltonic revaluation. The first three books, forming the first unit, are built upon the *concilia deorum*[2] and splits into two parts: the false and the true council of the gods. In the false council are lodged the descent to the underworld, the catalogue of heroes, and the epic journey, all of which exemplify the 'hybris' of the pagan heroes in their attempts to learn the future, make war, and assert their self-glorification and sometimes that of their people by travelling and invading. What Milton elevates in each of these two parallel scenes is the rational side of the classical world, of which the council is the fullest expression: we may remember that Phoenix told Achilles to be 'a speaker of words and a doer of deeds' (*Il.* IX, 443). Allotting so much time to councils – almost a third of the poem – and having the Father and the Son participate in this convention are ways of elevating and approving the convention, even though Satan abuses it. Later when Abdiel breaks with Satan in another council, we can see further the possibilities that exist for true heroic action in such a classical situation. Rhetoric and logic, abused by Satan and elevated by the Father and by the Son, receive approval in the council.

In the first classical unit, Milton used a common epic device and gave it as much approbation as Homer and Virgil, but in the second unit, Books IV and V (till l. 561), Milton expands considerably: the concern with the Golden World that preceded the world of epic battle. Homer gave us a glimpse of the fabled paradise in the gardens of Alcinoös, and Virgil carried on the tradition with the New Arcadia that Evander tried to create on the site of Rome, but these poets used paradise only as a backdrop to the strife-torn present, a nostalgic reminder of what had passed. Even the pastoral world that stands behind the fall of Troy is far from clear, although there is little point in elaborating upon a paradise that is lost forever, but in Milton, where man has the possibility of bringing back the age of gold, albeit inside himself, the pre-epic world has need of further development. In *Paradise Lost*, the loss of paradise is directly relevant to the evil that is present in the world today, so that understanding the past is a key to future happiness, rather than, as in the classical epic, a gloomy reminder of the whims of destiny: in the classical world, one cannot hope for much beyond the grave.

The third major unit is the war in heaven, a unit that includes many of the conventions of epic battles, such as flyting, the premature epic boast, the council of war, and the divine chariot of paternal power. Raphael shows Adam the consequences of those wars begun out of 'hybris' and out of disobedience to God. But warfare in general is shrunk to a column in the classical temple whereas once it covered the whole wall. The major source of classical heroism, at least in the *Iliad* and the *Aeneid*, is thereby diminished in importance. When the bard begins the second half of his poem,[3] he says, 'Half yet remains unsung, but narrower bound/ Within the visible Diurnal sphere' (VII, 21–2). Milton seems to be echoing Virgil who, at the same point in the poem, breaks in with a similar announcement of his second half of his poem: 'maior rerum mihi nascitur ordo,/ maius opus moueo' (VII, 44–5; 'A greater order of events opens for me; I begin a greater work'). The echo signals a change in structure, however, not a parallel: Virgil has completed the half of his poem that imitated the *Odyssey* and he is about to begin the part that imitates the *Iliad*: that is, he is about to shift to the martial section of the poem, just the reverse of what Milton is doing. Milton signals the shift away from battle, as the norm of epic heroism.

The next book expands one of the smallest details of the *Aeneid*, Iopas' song of creation (I, 740–6), into the fourth major structural unit of *Paradise Lost*. As the classical epic stressed battle narrative, Milton's epic lessened that stress and balanced destruction with creation:[4] the two books that tell of the creation of the world and of human beings. The emphasis upon war is not only contracted; it is criticized, and then replaced with the creative acts of God. The epic, through the addition of Christian values, has now become less the epic of death and more the epic of life, and the creative power of God is extended by the creative power that God placed in man, the power to change and develop, as Adam does in the succeeding books.

The struggle between the old epic and the new seems almost at times the struggle between life and death: Adam must die the old death before he can attain the new life. The fifth unit, Books IX and X, is the tragedy which Milton placed at the same point in the plot as in the *Iliad* and fortified with Homeric echoes in order to remind us that his epic is tragic too and that Adam and Eve must extricate themselves from the world of fallen pagan values. This escape needs the grace of God, without which Adam and Eve would remain, like Achilles and Patroklos, helpless in the course of the fatal consequences of sin.

The last unit, and last two books, is the vision of Michael, a vision which subsumes, transforms, and baptizes the classical epic and its philosophy into a synthesis of Christian and pagan values. Michael merges the conflicting worlds of classical and Christian epic, thereby ending one of the major conflicts in the poem. Yet it is significant that the vision includes the descent from heaven and the prophecy of the future that we find in classical epic. That this classical era is to be lived through and not ignored is exemplified by Michael's warrior's garb. What is important in the classical world and the classical epic is what the Christian can derive from them.

Although Milton used traditional epic conventions, he had to transform and reorder them from the classical epic, for his poem is the most optimistic of epics in spite of its tragic nature. The classical scenes with which the poem opens lead to the vision of Michael, through the *concilia deorum*, the pre-epic Golden World, the epic battle narrative, the narrative of the creation of the world and of man, and the epic tragedy. Throughout these conventions, we find balance and correction. The advocation of violence in the infernal council is balanced by the advocation of mercy in the celestial council; the battle in heaven, so swiftly swept away by the Son, is balanced by the extended accounts of creation which are preferable to destruction; and the paradisial world, though it falls into desolation, is partially restored by Michael's prophecy of a Savior coming to save man. The divine aspects of the poem perfectly balance the infernal and clearly triumph over them, while the human tragedy remains partially unresolved, for perfect restoration cannot come till the end of time and then it may not be universal. Hence the epic remains a tragedy for the human characters involved.

The expansions and contractions of the epic conventions dominating each unit are significant for Milton's revaluation of the classical epic. The importance of councils, the verbal, hence rational side of the epic, receives, as we saw, more emphasis than the martial, and the power of the godhead both in prophecy and creation is raised above its classical precedents. The expansion of the account of creation is the most drastic change from the classical epic. In short, more room is made for the power of the godhead in the Christian epic, though not without building upon Homer and Virgil. In the end, Adam and Eve, like the Christian reader, are left with vision and prophecy, two keys to Revelation and hence salvation.

In order to make the Christianization of the classical epic complete, Milton needed a new epic structure: the resemblance of the twelve books of the second edition of *Paradise Lost* to the twelve books of the *Aeneid* can be misleading: it is the contrast with the Virgilian epic that we are left with at the end of the poem: Virgil's epic, Milton reminds us, led to tragedy – it ends with the unheroic slaying of the suppliant, Turnus, an action contrary to Anchises' advice to 'spare the cast down' – and its hopes for the future were buried in the underworld in the middle of the poem. On the other hand, the Homeric epic led to reconciliations: in the *Iliad*, Achilles releases the body of Hector to Priam while, in the *Odyssey*, Odysseus restores order to Ithaka. But Milton's epic ends when Troy is being destroyed: his characters are just beginning their flight from the city of destruction and they have a longer and more difficult journey than Aeneas or Odysseus and a harder battle to fight than Achilles: they must avoid the pitfalls of classical egotism and find the gardens of Alcinoös inside themselves. For this task, they have only one advantage over their classical counterparts: the grace of God.

In addition to a new structure, Milton also needed a style that could at once invoke and revamp the classical tradition. I shall not discuss the controversies over Milton's 'Latinate' style but only point out some things that have not been said but which help to give the impression of a classical style in *Paradise Lost*.[5] Milton's method of elevating the language is the common one suggested by Aristotle: vary, within reason, the mode of normal speech by using unfamiliar words, figures, unusual forms and spellings, and, most of all, metaphors.[6] Through this method, Milton produced a variety of styles in *Paradise Lost*, but, as always, the classical epic appears in the background, from the Homeric directness of the Father to the Virgilianism of Raphael and the narrator. Yet within this variety, we may still talk of one style for the poem and see how it reflects the classical epic.

Like other Renaissance poets, Milton realized, after the work of the Earl of Surrey's translation of two books of the *Aeneid*, Spenser's *Faerie Queene*, and Shakespeare's tragedies, that iambic pentameter was the English equivalent of the classical dactylic hexameter He knew also that rhyme was not part of the classical epic and need not be part of the English epic either. What Milton wanted was an English style that could get closer to the flavor of classical epic, particularly Virgil's. The accomplishing of this task solidified the masonry of his Christian temple, for his epic merges Christian subject matter with a classical style that gives texture to even the most biblical passages in *Paradise Lost*. More than anything else. *Paradise Lost* is a triumph of style and the best example in English of what the classical epic style is like.

In order to increase the weight of the pentameter and make it sound more like the heavier hexameter with its occasional spondees, Milton increases the secondary accents with rhythmic regularity as in:

> Öf Mán's Fírst Dĭsŏbédiĕnce, ănd thĕ Frúit
> Öf thát Fŏrbíddĕn Trée, whŏse mórtăl tăste
> Brŏught Déath íntŏ thĕ Wórld, ănd áll oŭr wóe,
> Wĭth lóss ŏf Édĕn, tíll óne gréatĕr Mán
> Rĕstóre ús, ănd rĕgaín thĕ blíssfŭl Séat (I, 1–5).

Thus Milton's lines often seem to have more weight than five beats and come closer to the six-beat classical line of Homer and Virgil. The long formalized speeches in *Paradise Lost* also contribute to this effect; here Milton had to follow Virgil's verse paragraph rather than imitate Homer's verse which falls into units of one or two lines.[7] The heavy use of Homeric formulae are only useful in true oral epic, while Milton's poem, although it was composed orally because of the blindness of the poet, is intended to be read. The use of repeated epithets, phrases, and even whole speeches that we find in Homer would not suit Milton's audience who were attuned to Shakespeare and Spenser. The movement of the sense over the verse line is Virgilian, as is the technique of holding a key word till the end of a sentence or till the next line so when the word appears it changes the tone or even the meaning. So Milton holds back the word 'erring' in the following passage on the fall of Mulciber:

> from Morn
> To Noon he fell, from Noon to dewy Eve,
> A Summer's day; and with the setting Sun

Dropt from the Zenith like a falling Star,
On *Lemnos* th' *Aegean* Isle: thus they relate,
Erring (I, 742–7).

And Virgil withholds the word 'feruidus,' 'angry,' the word which signals the disapproval of the narrator of the slaying of Turnus by Aeneas and which points out that Aeneas is out of control: 'hoc dicens ferrum aduerso sub pectore condit/ feruidus' (XII, 950–1; 'Saying this he buries his sword in his enemy's breast angrily').

Sometimes Milton strives for the same effects that we find in Virgil, as when he gives Satan and his followers the following sibilant passage when they are turned into serpents: 'Thus was th' applause they meant/ Turn'd to exploding hiss, triumph to shame/ Cast on themselves from their own mouths' (X, 545–7). When they eat the foul fruit, we can hear the spewing subtly echoed in the fricatives and plosives of the following passage:

The Fruitage fair to sight, like that which grew
Near that bituminous Lake where *Sodom* flam'd;
This more delusive, not the touch, but taste
Deceiv'd; they fondly thinking to allay
Thir appetite with gust, instead of Fruit
Chew'd bitter Ashes, which th' offended taste
With spattering noise rejected (X, 561–7).

Here are Virgil's serpents hissing like spitting flames as they churn up the water:[8]

pectora quorum inter fluctus arrecta iubaeque
sanguineae superant undas, pars cetera pontum
pone legit sinuatque immensa uolumine terga,
fit sonitus spumante salo (II, 206–9).

In diction, Milton could echo Homer as well as Virgil, as in his delight in proper names in series or in specific words such as 'buxom' ('unreluctant') which Milton applies to air (II, 842; V, 270) and is his echoing of the Homeric formula '*οὐκ ἀέκοντε*' (e.g., *Il.* V, 366, 768) which refers to the horses of a chariot of the gods flying through the air. 'Labor' (II, 262, 1021), a key word in the *Aeneid* which expresses the suffering of man, finds a similar meaning in *Paradise Lost*, if we recall its Virgilian overtone, as does 'lapse,' meaning 'fall' (XII, 83), a noun in Milton which is cognate with Virgil's verb 'labor' (e.g., *Aen*. III, 309). When Adam speaks of opposing his 'obvious breast' to evil (XI, 374), it does not have its English sense of 'exposed' or 'in the way' (*OED*), but it has the Virgilian sense of 'hostilely confronting.'[9] These echoes are not just Latinisms or Graecisms but key words brought in from the classical epic in order to emulate and change it. For instance, Milton uses 'ruin' as a verb, 'Heav'n ruining from Heav'n' (VI, 868), or a noun, 'with hideous ruin' (I, 46),[10] often suggesting the destruction attendant upon military failure, but in Virgil, 'ruo' is often used of a soldier rushing into battle (e.g., X, 756; XI, 461; XII, 279; XII, 369; XII, 443; XII, 526). The shift in emphasis subtly reflects Milton's critical attitude towards purely martial valor.

Another technique besides echoing, though related to it, is ambiguity. I pointed out earlier the sinister joking that Milton picked up from Homer's doomed Patroklos and gave to Satan and Beelzebub, a technique that caused Walter Savage Landor to remark that the first sin of the fallen angels was punning.[11] We should also keep in mind Satan's offer to Eve to 'be as Gods' (IX, 708). This unfruitful ambiguity has its parallel in a fruitful ambiguity that gathers in both biblical and classical overtones and helps to synthesize the conflicts between the two worlds in the poem. Milton selects with great care words that apply to both worlds, so that 'thunder' and 'chariot' link pagan and Christian into one world view; sometimes Milton avoids terms that would be exclusively biblical or classical.

Such fruitful merging may be seen in the word 'wrath' which usually refers to divine retribution in *Paradise Lost*: 'So spake the Son, and into terror chang'd/ His count'nance too severe to be beheld/ And full of wrath bent on his Enemies' (VI, 824–6); 'headlong themselves they threw/ Down from the verge of heav'n, Eternal wrath/ Burn'd after them to the bottomless pit' (VI, 864–6). Satan, Gabriel, and Adam, after he falls, use the word to refer to divine retribution also, though the reader of classical epic is apt to remember it as a key word in the *Aeneid* and the Homeric poems, *wrath* being the usual equivalent of 'ira' in Latin and '*μῆνις*' in Greek. In the *Aeneid*, we find the initial conflict to be between the will of fate and 'saeuae memorem Iunonis . . . iram' (I, 4; 'the ever mindful wrath of angry Juno'). The same word 'ira' is the word for wrath in the Vulgate (e.g. Rev. VI: 16; XI: 18) and was usually Englished as such, as by Milton in his translations of the Psalms (e.g., II: 10, 27; LXXX: 19; LXXXV: 11; LXXXVIII: 65).

The word then partakes of both traditions and helps solidify

Milton's link between Virgil and the Bible. It also helps connect that link with Homer, for the theme of the *Iliad* is the wrath of Achilles: *'Μῆνιν ἄειδε, θεά, Πηληϊάδεω 'Αχιλῆος'* (I, 1), which Chapman translated 'Achilles' baneful wrath resound, O Goddesse'[12] and which Milton himself refers to as 'the wrath/ Of stern *Achilles*' (IX, 14–15). Unlike 'ira,' *'μῆνις'* usually refers to the wrath of the gods, especially in the *Odyssey* (e.g. II, 66; V, 146; and XIV, 283), a usage that Milton reminds us of by transferring it back to God. Milton follows Homer in suggesting the inappropriateness of wrath in any other hands. Achilles and Juno are peevish, and their wrath is based upon revenge, not justice. The word is not used of Satan in *Paradise Lost*, and only one other time does it refer to anyone else besides the Father, the Son, or Achilles: it is used once of Death, when he, 'full of wrath,' assaults Satan (II, 688). But Sin reminds him that his wrath is futile, since it is inferior to God's:

> For him who sits above and laughs the while
> At thee ordain'd his drudge, to execute
> Whate'er his wrath, which he calls Justice, bids,
> His wrath which one day will destroy ye both (II, 731–4).

Unlike the pagan deities, the Father can put aside His wrath which gradually yields to grace and mercy. Adam senses this mollification in the words of the judging Son: he tells Eve that the Son 'both heard and judg'd/ Without wrath or reviling' (X, 1047–8). By the end of the poem, Adam learns that God's wrath shall lead to good: 'that much more good thereof shall spring,/ To God more glory, more good will to Men/ From God, and over wrath grace shall abound' (XII, 476–8). The wrath of the pagan gods and heroes is now transcended by the grace and glory of God; that wrath has merged with the wrath of the God of the Bible, and that wrath too has been transcended.

'Wrath' has been transformed into 'glory,' another key word that links the pagan and the Christian worlds. In the seventeenth century, 'glory' had already become a staple of hymns and prayers. In Milton's epic, it is a major attribute of God:

> Glory they sung to the most High, good will
> To future men, and in their dwellings peace:
> Glory to him whose just avenging ire
> Had driven out th' ungodly from his sight
> And th' habitations of the just; to him
> Glory and praise (VII, 182–7).

Glory encompasses many overlapping meanings in *Paradise Lost*: happiness, praise, fame, splendor, and the light of the 'aureola' or 'nimbus.' It is particularly the element of God that is reflected in his creatures and creation, so the Son is the 'radiant image of his Glory' (III, 63), Raphael appears as 'glorious' (V, 309, 362), Adam and Eve possess 'the image of thir glorious Maker' (IV, 292), and they sing of the 'glorious' works of God (IV, 658; V, 153). This glory of creatures is contingent so Satan and Adam lose it when they fall (IV, 838; X, 722) and cannot regain it without God's help.

As Michael reminds Adam, glory was wrested from God during the classical era and transferred to the conquering hero:

> For in those days Might only shall be admir'd
> And Valor and Heroic Virtue call'd;
> To overcome in Battle, and subdue
> Nations, and bring home spoils with infinite
> Man-slaughter, shall be held the highest pitch
> Of human Glory, and for Glory done
> Of triumph, to be styl'd great Conquerors,
> Patrons of Mankind, Gods and Sons of Gods,
> Destroyers rightlier call'd and Plagues of men (XI, 689–97).

Like 'wrath,' 'glory' is a key word in the epic tradition.[13] In Homer, the word appears in its cognates '*κλέος*' and '*κλείω*' and refers to heroic actions that are celebrated by the bards, so Achilles sings the '*κλέα ἀνδρῶν*' (*Il.* IX, 189), 'the glorious deeds of men,' and Penelope speaks of ' "the deeds of men and gods which the bards glorify" ' (*Od.* I, 338: '*ἔργ' ἀνδρῶν τε θεῶν τε, τά τε κλείουσιν ἀοιδοί*'). Though he often prefers 'fama,' Virgil uses 'gloria' in this heroic sense too, as when Sinon claims to have served Palamedes, a man whose glory and fame were renowned: 'nomen Palamedis et incluta fama/ gloria' (II, 82–3). Virgil's use of 'incluta' which is related to Homer's '*κλείω*' is a good example of epic echoing and shows Milton's method as well as Virgil's. In addition, Aeneas and Turnus both speak of the 'gloria' of their heroic peoples (VI, 65; XI, 431).

In *Paradise Lost*, Satan arrogates glory to himself in the classical sense of the word: for Satan, it is the hero's reward for valorous action. So Satan speaks of the 'Glorious Enterprise' of the war in heaven (I, 89), a war that shall be renewed and in the second attempt 'will appear/ More glorious' (II, 15–16), since they will be fighting with the disadvantage of the once defeated. Like Aeneas and Turnus, Satan 'glories' in the greatness of his followers (I, 573). He tells Abdiel that glory is the reward for deeds of battle and that the pursuit of glory is an end in itself and not to be measured by moral yardsticks: 'The strife which thou call'st evil, but wee style/ The strife of Glory' (VI, 289–90). Satan also adopts the pagan attitude that the quality of one's foe raises the level of the glory to be derived from the encounter, as Satan tells Gabriel:

> If I must contend, said he,
> Best with the best, the Sender not the sent,
> Or all at once; more glory will be won,
> Or less be lost (IV, 851–4).

Satan debases the concept of pagan glory however, when, after his defeat, he resorts to revenge in Eden and that upon unequals: 'To mee shall be the glory sole among/ Th' infernal Powers, in one day to have marr'd/ What he *Almighty* styl'd six Nights and Days' (IX, 135–7). As always, Satan represents degenerate classical values, as when he boasts of his 'glorious Work' to Sin and Death (X, 391) and tells them that he can now 'glorie' in the name of heaven's 'Antagonist' (X, 386–7) and that his work will now be extended by the 'glorious march' of his children to earth (X, 474). The glory that Satan hands over is now as debased as the notion of the hero's offspring taking over his kingdom.

The same arrogation of glory belongs to Eve at the time of the fall. She transfers the glory of her being to herself rather than seeing it as a reflection of the glory of God, just as Satan told Abdiel that the angels were not created by God but that 'Our puissance is our own' (V, 864). Eve, like Satan battling against God, sees Adam's defiance of the commandment as a 'glorious trial' (IX, 961), a notion reflected in the fallen Adam who uses the same expression later (IX, 1177) in order to mock Eve's self-styled heroism. Adam may have remembered Raphael's lesson on the vanity of personal glory in his description of the war in heaven:

> I might relate of thousands, and thir names
> Eternize here on Earth; but those elect
> Angels contented with thir fame in Heav'n
> Seek not the praise of men; the other sort
> In might though wondrous and in Acts of War,
> Nor of Renown less eager, yet by doom
> Cancell'd from Heav'n and sacred memory,
> Nameless in dark oblivion let them dwell.
> For strength from Truth divided and from Just,
> Illaudable, naught merits but dispraise
> And ignominy, yet to glory aspires

> Vain-glorious, and through infamy seeks fame:
> Therefore Eternal silence be thir doom (VI, 373–85).

True glory stems from obedience to God, so that Abdiel gains fame and glory from God because he defeats Satan out of his love of God, not self. As a result, the Father promises that Abdiel will return 'more glorious' (VI, 39) on his enemies because he has fought the 'better fight' (VI, 30), for the glory of God, not for the glory of classical heroism.

As the glory of classical heroism diminishes, the glory of God increases in *Paradise Lost*. As Raphael points out, the war in heaven is the 'ruin of so many glorious once' (V, 567). Later when Satan appears before his followers in order to announce his successes in Eden, he appears as 'thir glorious Chief' (X, 537), but only to be cast down by God. The glory that Satan is left with is a 'permissive glory' that is only a 'false glitter' now (X, 451–2) because, as he himself knows, 'I fell, how glorious once' (IV, 39). Adam and Eve too lose their glory and must don clothes to cover up the loss of 'that first naked Glory' (IX, 1115).

Later will appear the mistaken glory of the classical epic, but Adam and the reader too must remember that Michael, the 'glorious Apparition' (XI, 211), is a reflection of God, as all true epic heroes are, Christian and pagan alike – for the pagan heroes are models of behavior, if we read them correctly, in both their virtues and their faults. At the close of the poem, Michael displaces the classical heroes by showing Adam that there is 'glory' in the behavior of Moses and in Aaron's leading of the Jews back to the Promised Land (XII, 172). It is not Augustus, but Christ, as we saw earlier, who will bound His 'glory with the heav'ns' (XII, 371) and 'enter into Glory' (XII, 456), while He captures Satan and takes away his glory forever and judges 'with glory and power' (XII, 460). Only the Son will gain the fame till now given to epic heroes, only His name will be 'exalted high/ Above all names in Heav'n' (XII, 457–8). Then Christian glory will outshine pagan wrath:

> Now amplier known thy Savior and thy Lord,
> Last in the Clouds from Heav'n to be reveal'd
> In glory of the Father, to dissolve
> *Satan* with his perverted World (XII, 544–7).

So Adam: 'To God more glory, more good will to Men/ From God, and over wrath grace shall abound' (XII, 477–8).

Beside diction, one of the most characteristic features of the epic style is the epic simile, a subject that has received a good deal of critical attention.[14] I do not intend to add to the general conception of the Miltonic simile but to make some new and closer connections with its classical predecessors. The epic simile usually begins with 'as,' 'ὥς,' or 'ut' and often adds 'thus' or 'so,' or equivalents in Greek and Latin. It adds depth or variety to the action. Homer was the master of the simile, even though he often digressed in his comparisons, so that Virgil, as is well known, developed the compressed simile rather than compete with Homer's variety. We might have noticed earlier that the simile was Satan's calling card; when he enters Eden, Milton uses two similes:

> As when a prowling Wolf,
> Whom hunger drives to seek new haunt for prey,
> Watching where Shepherds pen thir Flocks at eve
> In hurdl'd Cotes amid the field secure,
> Leaps o'er the fence with ease into the Fold:
> Or as a Thief bent to unhoard the cash
> Of some rich Burgher, whose substantial doors,
> Cross-barr'd and bolted fast, fear no assault,
> In at the window climbs, or o'er the tiles;
> So clomb this first grand Thief into God's Fold (IV, 183–92).

The first simile, as Bush notes in his edition of Milton, resembles Virgil's:

> Ac ueluti pleno lupus insidiatus ouili
> cum fremit ad caulas uentos perpessus et imbris
> nocte super media; tuti sub matribus agni
> balatum exercent, ille asper et improbus ira
> saeuit in absentis; collecta fatigat edendi
> ex longo rabies et siccae sanguine fauces:
> haud aliter Rutulo muros et castra tuenti
> ignescunt irae, duris dolor ossibus ardet (IX, 59–66).

> (Just as when a wolf lying in ambush at a full sheepfold howls at the enclosures, enduring wind and rain at midnight; safe beneath their mothers, the lambs keep bleating; he, cruel and monstrous in his wrath, rages at those he cannot see; the long-gathered rage for food and his jaws, dry of blood, torture him: not otherwise does wrath burn the Rutulian when he sees the walls and camp; anguish glows in his hard bones.)

It is also Virgilian in form: the wolf clearly referring to Satan, as Virgil's wolf referred to Turnus, and the pastoral victims referring to Adam and Eve and their descendants, just as Virgil's sheep are the Trojans without Aeneas. The pastoral nature of Eden and its fence of bristling woods make the simile fit the situation very snugly. The second simile possibly originates in the *Iliad* (III, 10–14) where the dust that the two armies stir up is likened to the mist that hides the robber; but whatever its origin, it is Homeric in its expansion of details: the cash corresponds to the happiness that Adam and Eve share in paradise, but the doors, bars, bolts, window, and tiles do not have corresponding meanings in the simile, though the robber is both a degradation of Satanic heroism and a consequence of Satan's triumph in the garden. Indeed, modern criticism has shown that correspondences between the elements in a Miltonic simile and the elements of the plot are sometimes either remote or difficult to detect. For instance, who is the plowman in the simile used to describe Gabriel's guards as they move towards Satan in Eden?[15]

> With ported Spears, as thick as when a field
> Of *Ceres* ripe for harvest waving bends
> Her bearded Grove of ears, which way the wind
> Sways them; the careful Plowman doubting stands
> Lest on the threshing floor his hopeful sheaves
> Prove chaff (IV, 980–5).

It seems that there is no need to look for Virgilian economy and exact correspondence here, especially when we remember that Homer sometimes places a human figure in his nature similes. For example, when the two Ajaxes drive on the troops to battle, Homer compares the scene to the west wind driving black clouds across the sea and adds the goatherd who watches from the shore, then rises in fear, and drives his goats into a cave:

> *ὡς δ' ὅτ' ἀπὸ σκοπιῆς εἶδεν νέφος αἰπόλος ἀνὴρ*
> *ἐρχόμενον κατὰ πόντον ὑπὸ Ζεφύροιο ἰωῆς·*
> *τῷ δέ τ' ἄνευθεν ἐόντι μελάντερον ἠΰτε πίσσα*
> *φαίνετ' ἰὸν κατὰ πόντον, ἄγει δέ τε λαίλαπα πολλήν,*
> *ῥιγησέν τε ἰδών, ὑπό τε σπέος ἤλασε μῆλα* (IV, 275–9).

> (Just as when, from his outlook the goatherd discovers a storm cloud coming over the sea from roaring Zephyrus. To him being far off, it seems blacker than pitch, as it moves on the sea and drives on the great whirlwind. Seeing this he trembles and drives his herd under a cavern.)

Another Homeric element in the Miltonic simile is the inclusion of the everyday world in the epic poem: the simple plowman and the goatherd remind us of the world of peace that is being destroyed in each poem.[16]

The piling up of similes, pick-a-back, as when Satan enters Eden above – there are really three similes if we add the next line to IV, 183–92 – is both Virgilian and Homeric. Such similes compare Aeneas' and Turnus' raging at one another first to a fire and then to a mountain torrent (XII, 521–5; cf. *Il.* XIV, 394–401).

Most aspects of the Miltonic simile therefore reflect both Homeric and Virgilian elements, such as the comparing of great things to small without any loss of grandeur, the danger of such similes being that the smallness of the thing to which the subject is being compared will lower the subject rather than elevate it by understatement. The three major epic poets succeed however: Homer compares a warrior's courage to that of a house-fly that audaciously bites a man who is shooing him away (*Il.* XVII, 570–2); Virgil compares the builders of Carthage to bees busily pursuing their labors (I, 430–6); and Milton compares Satan and his legions to the pygmies, 'that small infantry/ Warr'd on by Cranes' (I, 575–6).[17]

Besides such examples of *contaminatio* and *retractatio*, we find Milton improvising and transforming the simile. Sometimes we find epic emulation, as when Satan's shield is likened to the moon while Hector's is likened only to a star (*Il.* XI, 62–3). Sometimes there is an added significance, as when the robber that Satan is compared to is a result of Satan's entry into Eden in the first place. Sometimes the simile turns into reality as when Satan actually becomes the wild beasts familiar from epic similes:

> A Lion now he stalks with fiery glare,
> Then as a Tiger, who by chance hath spi'd
> In some Purlieu two gentle fawns at play,
> Straight couches close, then rising changes oft
> His couchant watch, as one who chose his ground
> Whence rushing he might surest seize them both
> Gript in each paw (IV, 402–8).

This passage is more than a simile since it is a real metamorphosis of Satan into these beasts. Later we find the similes in Homer and Virgil, where we find also the world of predatory animal life that began with the fall. As we saw earlier, the ferocious world of the epic simile begins after the fall (XI, 185–90).

Milton makes use of another device that is only latent in the classical epic poets. In *Paradise Lost*, the similes belong to the human narrator, not to the secondary narrator, as in the *Aeneid* where Aeneas tells the tale within the tale:[18] Raphael makes only one simile (VI, 856–8), while the final epic narrator, Michael, makes none nor do the other human or divine characters in the poem. Tension arises between the classical narrative voice, the voice that creates similes, and the other angelic narrators who do not rely upon the classical simile as much, but the simile is not discarded. Like the other elements in the poem, style too modifies the classical epic till it can merge with Christianity. The form of the classical epic simile remains but it is gradually infused with biblical subject matter. Raphael's only simile is a good example: he compares the driving out of the rebel angels from heaven by the Son to 'a Herd/ Of Goats or timorous flock together throng'd' (VI, 856–7). The familiar classical elements are there – the herd of goats, the violence, and the pastoral world – but the real frame of reference is the Bible as Hughes notes, particularly that passage where it is prophesied by a simile that the Son will come to judge the world:

> And before him shalbe gathered all nacions, and he shal separate them one from another, as a shepherde separateth the shepe from the goates (Matt. XXV: 32; The Geneva Bible).

That the Bible too has similes helps Milton's Christian and pagan synthesis. Just as Michael led Adam to the Scriptures just after he had fallen into the world of pagan epic represented by Satan, so Raphael leads to the Bible after his Homeric account of the war in heaven.

When the epic similes appear again at the end of *Paradise Lost*, they no longer lead to specific epic sources nor do they seem specifically Homeric or Virgilian:

> The Cherubim descended; on the ground
> Gliding meteorous, as Ev'ning Mist
> Ris'n from a River o'er the marish glides,
> And gathers ground fast at the Laborer's heel
> Homeward returning. High in Front advanc't,
> The brandisht Sword of God before them blaz'd
> Fierce as a Comet; which with torrid heat,
> And vapor as the *Libyan* Air adust,
> Began to parch that temperate Clime (XII, 628–36).

As with the resemblance of the destruction of Eden to the fall of Troy, the classical allusions are further in the background. There has been a displacement rather than a clear allusion. When Satan's legions lay scattered like fallen leaves the reader is immediately invited to think of the appropriate passages in Homer and Virgil. In the distant background here lies an allusion to the simile of Achilles as the fatal star which brings destruction to Troy as the sword above is a comet blazing destruction over Eden. The Bible, however, has the more relevant context: 'but a mist went up from the earth and watered the whole face of the ground' (Gen. II: 6) and

> He drove out the man; and at the east of the garden of Eden he placed the cherubim, and a flaming sword which turned every way, to guard the way to the tree of life (Gen. III: 24).

The classical allusions now take a more humble place in the epic, as the classics themselves had to with the coming of Christianity. Yet they remain. The narrator does not have the purity of God's word nor the pristine innocence of Eden but the balance has been righted. If the Son of God in *Paradise Regained* can learn to shun all classical learning, the human narrator cannot, for the classical epic still has something to teach him and in his search for truth he can neglect nothing.

The epic voice behind these stylistic devices is the most dramatic of Milton's adaptations and breaks with the epic tradition, although it has gone unnoticed.[19] In many of the changes that we have seen, as in the descent, the vision, and the hero, Milton adapted the classical epic to the needs of a true Christian epic through his own methods. There was little reason however to change the impersonal bard of the classical epic into the personal narrator for theological consistency. In his *Poetics*, Aristotle praises Homer for his reticence, because it is consistent with his role as imitator.[20] Following his mentor, Virgil keeps his own voice low and thus sets the precedent for the rest of the tradition. The social nature of early epic, the fact that it represented the history of a people, no doubt was a cause of this impersonality in the narrator. But in the seventeenth century, the individual voice was being heard in the lyric, and Milton tells us that autobiography is not out of place in poetry as it is in prose: 'a poet, soaring in the high region of his fancies with his garland and singing robes about him might without apology speak more of himself than I mean to do [in prose]' (I, 808).

This development in the epic narrator is gradual. At first, he is the closest link with the epic tradition; whether he himself is learned or is the means by which the Holy Spirit operates is here immaterial. He brings in the classical allusions in a purer form than any other narrator in the poem, though, as we saw, his style becomes 'purified' of some of its classicism. He composes the similes that send us back to the classical poets; he adopts the melancholy tone of Virgil and Homer, he alludes to Virgil's half-way point in the story, he sides with certain characters, though religious considerations forbid him to sympathize with Satan and his followers in the way that Homer and Virgil could sympathize with their villains, and like Homer (e.g. *Il.* XV, 365–6) he pays respect to the divinities. He maintains part of the objectivity of the classical bard by never addressing the audience but only the muse, God, and the characters, the last being addressed sparingly. He also shares the classical penchant for foreshadowing, flashbacks, and mythological references.

The narrator's foreshadowing of events is one way Milton revaluates the epic tradition. This technique has been noticed before, though not commented upon in general.[21] An epic narrator always begins his poem by telling the outcome of the action: the wrath of Achilles sent many Achaians to their graves, Odysseus returned home, and man fell through disobedience. During the poem lesser events are foreshadowed by the intervention of the bard: when Patroklos asks Achilles if he can go into battle, the bard tells us that Patroklos is entreating his own death (XVI, 46–7), and, when Hector slays Patroklos, the bard again enters to say that Hector's own death is not far off (XVI, 800). In the *Odyssey*, the narrator adds an aside during the test of the bow that Antinoös, the most unruly of the suitors, will be the first to die when Odysseus later turns the bow into an instrument of revenge (XXI, 98–100) and the death of the suitors is forecast throughout the poem. In the *Aeneid*, we are told, when we meet her, that Dido will die (I, 712) and when Pallas and Lausus meet on the battlefield, Virgil tells us that neither lived to return home (X, 435–6).

Foreshadowing is linked in the pagan epics to the sense of doom that pervades those poems: as Jupiter tells us in the *Aeneid*: ' "stat sua cuique dies, breue et inreparabile tempus/ omnibus est uitae" ' (X, 467–8; ' "each man has his day; the time of life is short for all men and irrecoverable" '). Even prophecies such as Anchises' and Teiresias' often have this sense of doom. Milton continues this tradition by foreshadowing the fall both directly and indirectly. At the beginning of the tragic Book IX, he announces that he will shortly sing of 'foul distrust, and breach/ Disloyal on the part of Man, revolt/ And disobedience' (IX, 6–8). Sometimes the forecasting is subtle: the bard tells us that Eden is so beautiful that it is not to be compared to

> that fair field
> Of *Enna*, where *Proserpin* gath'ring flow'rs
> Herself a fairer Flow'r by gloomy *Dis*
> Was gather'd, which cost *Ceres* all that pain (IV, 268–71).

But the sense of doom shifts after the fall to the positive prophecy of the seed of the woman's crushing the head of the serpent. Thus foreshadowing is turned to something Christian and, because it involves the undoing of Satan's work in the garden, life-giving.

Related to foreshadowing but far more controversial is the habit of authorial intrusion in Milton, as when the poet comments upon a character: 'So spake th' Apostate Angel, though in pain,/ Vaunting aloud, but rackt with deep despair' (I, 125–6). This habit Milton has been taken to task for, but, although such criticism has been adequately answered, no one has yet pointed out the classical precedent for authorial intrusion.[22] Yet such comment is common in the epic tradition. Homer comments, as we have seen, upon Agamemnon's easy confidence in the deceptive dream that Zeus sent in order to delude the commander into believing that Troy could now be taken:

> *νήπιος, οὐδὲ τὰ ᾔδη ἅ ῥα Ζεὺς μήδετο ἔργα·*
> *θήσειν γὰρ ἔτ' ἔμελλεν ἐπ' ἄλγεά τε στοναχάς τε*
> *Τρωσί τε καὶ Δαναοῖσι διὰ κρατερὰς ὑσμίνας* (II, 38–40).
>
> (Fool, he did not know what plans Zeus devised; he was still to cause pain and groaning to Trojans and Danaans alike in the hard battles.)

Similarly Virgil interjects when Turnus takes Pallas' belt off his corpse: 'nescia mens hominum fati sortisque futurae/ et seruare modum rebus sublata secundis' (X, 501–2; 'how the mind of man is unmindful of fate and future destiny and of remaining temperate when elevated by favorable events!'). In all three epics the bard reserves the right to break the fiction for dramatic effect.

The epic poet does not stop at intrusion, however, he sometimes addresses his characters directly through apostrophe. Homer freely but infrequently addresses his characters, especially the Greeks in the *Iliad*: eight times he bursts in to call to Patroklos out of sympathy, as we have already seen, and once he calls the dead Melanippos, as Antilochos rushes to strip off his armor:

> *ὣς ἐπὶ σοί, Μελάνιππε, θόρ' 'Αντίλοχος μενεχάρμης*
> *τεύχεα συλήσων· ἀλλ' οὐ λάθεν ''Εκτορα δῖον,*
> *ὅς ῥά οἱ ἀντίος ἦλθε θέων ἀνὰ δηϊοτῆτα* (XV, 582–4).

> (Thus upon you, Melanippos, steadfast Antilochos leapt to strip off your armor but did not escape the notice of godlike Hector, who then came rushing through the slaughter against him.)

Seven times the poet calls to Menelaos, three times out of fear for his life (IV, 127, 146; VII, 105); the other four times Menelaos is praised for his courage (XIII, 604; XVII, 679, 702) and his humanity (XXIII, 600). Once he addresses Achilles (XX, 2). Considering the length of the *Iliad*, Homer uses this device with Hellenic restraint [23]

The same motives, sympathy and the desire to praise, cause Virgil's even more infrequent outbursts: he admires Camilla's daring (XI, 664–5) and sympathizes with Dido (IV, 408–11), Palinurus (V, 840), Pallas (X, 507–9), Cretheus (XII, 538–9), Aeolus (XII, 542–7) and especially Nisus and Euryalus:

> Fortunati ambo! si quid mea carmina possunt,
> nulla dies umquam memori uos eximet aeuo,
> dum domus Aeneae Capitoli immobile saxum
> accolet imperiumque pater Romanus habebit (IX, 446–9).

> (Fortunate pair! if my poetry can do it, no day shall ever remove you from the memory of time as long as the House of Aeneas shall dwell by the immoveable rock of the Capitoline and the Roman father hold imperial power.)

Milton too addresses his characters, but he does not imitate the praise for martial behavior that we found in the two earlier poets; he only imitates their sympathy:

> How didst thou grieve then, *Adam*, to behold
> The end of all thy Offspring, end so sad,
> Depopulation; thee another Flood,
> Of tears and sorrow a Flood thee also drown'd,
> And sunk thee as thy Sons (XI, 754–8).

Milton's outburst is well timed: it backs up the relenting of God's anger and shows His grace coming to Adam as he learns through Michael to accept the consequences of his sin. But one outburst stands out above the others, another technique that derives from

Homer and Virgil. The center of Homer's addresses is really Patroklos who is addressed eight times by the poet, a natural development of the idea that Patroklos is the major sacrifice made for the Greeks as a consequence of the wrath of Achilles. In the *Aeneid*, the addresses call attention to Nisus and Euryalus, whose valor and friendship is one of the sacrifices that Rome must pay for empire. In *Paradise Lost*, the major address, as we have seen, is to Eve upon her departure from Adam:

> O much deceiv'd, much failing, hapless *Eve*,
> Of thy presum'd return! event perverse!
> Thou never from that hour in Paradise
> Found'st either sweet repast, or sound repose;
> Such ambush hid among sweet Flow'rs and Shades
> Waited with hellish rancor imminent
> To intercept thy way, or send thee back
> Despoil'd of Innocence, of Faith, of Bliss (IX, 404–11).

But the relationship between the bard and his characters has changed and intensified. Homer's sympathy is that of a poet who begins to believe in his own character, unlike Virgil who seems to have had some real people in mind. But the bard of *Paradise Lost* is about to watch the initial act of evil, the source of not only Eve's but 'all our woe,' including his own blindness. She also represents the whole race where Patroklos and the Roman pair did not. For this reason, he cannot give the sympathy to the anti-hero that Virgil could: Turnus is only a warrior, but Satan is evil itself. Milton is as far as possible from the universal sympathy that Homer affords, and Milton believes that he is that much closer to the truth.

On the other hand, Milton has intensified the relationship between the bard and the gods, another theme that is not so much a break with the epic tradition as a fulfillment of it. All three epic poets address deities; Homer addresses Apollo in the *Iliad*: '*ὥσ ῥα σύ, ἤϊε Φοῖβε, πολὺν κάματον καὶ ὀϊζὺν/σύγχεας Ἀργείων, αὐτοῖσι δὲ φύζαν ἐνῶρσας*' (XV, 365–6; 'thus you, glorious Apollo, confounded the great toil and suffering of the Argives and in them stirred up panic'; cf. XX, 152). The dominant emotion is fearful respect in the attitude of Homer. This attitude is echoed in Virgil's address to Jupiter: 'tanton placuit concurrere motu,/ Iuppiter, aeterna gentis in pace futuras?' (XII, 503–4; 'was it pleasing to you, Jupiter, that peoples later to live in eternal peace should clash together with such a great force?'). But the relationship seems closer between God and man in the *Aeneid*, for the wills of bard and godhead are more in agreement than in Homer. At one point the bard seems to join in a hymn to Hercules:

> 'tu nubigenas, inuicte, bimembris
> Hylaeumque Pholumque manu, tu Cresia mactas
> prodigia et uastum Nemeae sub rupe leonem.
> te Stygii tremuere lacus, te ianitor Orci
> ossa super recubans antro semesa cruento;
> nec te ullae facies, non terruit ipse Typhoeus
> arduus arma tenens; non te rationis egentem
> Lernaeus turba capitum circumstetit anguis.
> salue, uera Iouis proles, decus addite diuis,
> et nos et tua dexter adi pede sacra secundo' (VIII, 293–302).

> ('O you, unconquerable, you who killed by hand the double-limbed children of the clouds, Hylaeus and Pholus, the Cretan monsters and the great lion under the Nemean cliff. The Stygian lake and the porter of hell lying upon half-eaten bones in his bloody cave trembled at you: no sight appalled you, not Typhoeus himself holding his arms aloft; nor were you without presence of mind when the Lernean serpent surrounded you with its crowd of heads. Hail, true son of Jove, added as a grace to the gods, come to us and your rites, propitious with favoring foot.')

Milton's song to the Creator, a song in which narrator and angels join, is a natural development out of the epic tradition as well as a biblical embellishment. Psalm and epic hymn meet in a harmonic synthesis of pagan and Christian worship, which is in fact an outgrowth of the classical world:

> Thee Father first they sung Omnipotent,
> Immutable, Immortal, Infinite,
> Eternal King; thee Author of all being,
> Fountain of Light, thyself invisible
> Amidst the glorious brightness where thou sit'st
> . . . . .
> Thee next they sang of all Creation first,
> Begotten Son, Divine Similitude,
> . . . . .
> Hee Heav'n of Heavens and all the Powers therein
> By thee created, and by thee threw down
> Th' aspiring Dominations: thou that day
> Thy Father's dreadful Thunder didst not spare,
> Nor stop thy flaming Chariot wheels, that shook
> Heav'n's everlasting Frame, while o'er the necks

> Thou drov'st of warring Angels disarray'd (III, 372–6; 383–4; 390–6).

Virgil sang of Hercules as the true son of God but we find this idea countered here, though Hercules was sometimes a classical analogue of the true Son.[24] So far the hymn could be called almost pagan: it is the last part of this hymn which extends, like all of *Paradise Lost*, through and beyond the pagan world into the world of Christ. The last part of the hymn sings of the sacrifice of the Son on the cross as an example of God's love for man, an action beyond the theology of the classical epic:

> O unexampl'd love,
> Love nowhere to be found less than Divine!
> Hail Son of God, Savior of Men, thy Name
> Shall be the copious matter of my Song
> Henceforth, and never shall my Harp thy praise
> Forget, nor from thy Father's praise disjoin (III, 410–15).

The harp is the instrument both of Demodocus and of David.

The epic voice is not undivided in his pagan and classical interests, but he gradually develops towards the synthesis that Michael presents at the end of the poem. At the beginning, his invocations are balanced between Christian and pagan. He prays to the Holy Spirit that inspired Moses, but he thinks of the deity as inhabiting a place, like the pagan poets, as Gilbert Murray noticed:[25] 'or if *Sion* Hill/ Delight thee more; and *Siloa's* Brook' (I, 10–11). Moreover, like Satan, Adam, and Eve, he is presumptuous: they sinned through disobedience, he might be said to sin through the pride of epic emulation: his poem, 'with no middle flight intends to soar/ Above th' *Aonian* Mount, while it pursues/ Things unattempted yet in Prose or Rhyme' (I, 14–16).

But by the second invocation the bard begins to have doubts and worries lest he may say 'undecent things of the gods' (*Prose*, I, 891) like Homer: 'Hail holy Light . . . May I express thee unblam'd?' (III, 1, 3). He invokes other epic poets and blind bards but not just out of emulation:

> Those other two equall'd with me in Fate,
> So were I equall'd with them in renown,
> Blind *Thamyris* and blind *Maeonides*,
> And *Tiresias* and *Phineus* Prophets old (III, 33–6).

Such emulation is ambiguous for it carries with it its own warning. In legend Homer (Maeonides) was blind, poor, and unrewarded, perhaps being punished for his remarks upon the gods. Phineus was in disgrace for revealing the counsels of Zeus, and Teiresias was punished by Hera for seeing Athene bathing.[26] Thamyris was an arrogant Thracian bard who dared to challenge the muses in song and was blinded for his arrogance, a story that is told by Homer (*Il*. II, 594–600) and so remains a warning to later epic poets.

In the third invocation, the conflict increases. The narrator, once more like Homer, resorts to mythological lessons against presumption, but this time he does so directly;

> Return me to my Native Element:
> Lest from this flying Steed unrein'd (as once
> *Bellerophon*, though from a lower Clime)
> Dismounted, on th' *Aleian* Field I fall (VII, 16–19).

The narrator has become more conscious of the limitations of the classical muse and now elevates Urania, whose name means 'heavenly' to her true sphere above Mount Olympus, now shrunk to a 'hill':

> Descend from Heav'n *Urania*, by that name
> If rightly thou art call'd, whose Voice divine
> Following, above th' *Olympian* Hill I soar,
> Above the flight of *Pegasean* wing.
> The meaning not the Name I call; for thou
> Nor of the Muses nine, nor on the top
> Of old *Olympus* dwell'st, but Heav'nly born (VII, 1–7).

Like Adam, the narrator is learning the proper balance between Christian and pagan. Urania is relegated to being the power of God, as if the narrator were glossing a classical text. His purpose, like that of all the classical aspects of *Paradise Lost*, is to point to the divine origins of the best of the classical epic, while pointing to the human origins of its Satanism. The old relationship between the muse and the bard is dramatized and done away with by the reference to Orpheus, the symbol of the classical poet, who cannot be saved by Calliope, muse of epic poetry, chief of the nine muses, and mother of Orpheus:

> But drive far off the barbarous dissonance
> Of *Bacchus* and his Revellers, the Race
> Of that wild Rout that tore the *Thracian* Bard
> In *Rhodope*, where Woods and Rocks had Ears
> To rapture, till the savage clamor drown'd
> Both Harp and Voice; nor could the Muse defend

Her Son. So fail not thou, who thee implores:
For thou art Heav'nly, shee an empty dream (VII, 32–9).

The bard who turns to the Christian muse has a chance of being protected and saved, a result of his becoming more aware of the limitations of the classical epic. At this point, half way through the poem, he can reject the classical muse as an 'empty dream,' because he has gained perspective on the classical world through Satan's behavior and has seen through Urania to God. Like Adam, he too has learned something from Raphael's account of the war in heaven about the nature of true heroism.

This wider consciousness of the bard comes out in the next invocation which lowers the pagan epic in favor of the Christian epic and is, in part, a revaluation of some of what the poet has already composed:

Sad task, yet argument
Not less but more Heroic than the wrath
Of stern *Achilles* on his Foe pursu'd
Thrice Fugitive about *Troy* Wall; or rage
Of *Turnus* for *Lavinia* disespous'd,
Or *Neptune's* ire or *Juno's*, that so long
Perplex'd the *Greek* and *Cytherea's* Son (IX, 13–19).

Here Milton does not reject the epic tradition: that tradition still has its heroism but it is 'less heroic' than what emerges from man's struggles in his soul. The price of this true epic poem is the loss of the bard's own power; he must rely on

my Celestial Patroness, who deigns
Her nightly visitation unimplor'd,
And dictates to me slumb'ring, or inspires
Easy my unpremeditated Verse (IX, 21–4).

This is the muse that inspired Homer and Virgil at their best. Just as the warrior cannot take credit for his accomplishments neither can the epic bard, but he owes all to God, a fact dramatized in *Paradise Lost* by the bard's being twice relieved of his epic task when the account of the war in heaven and the vision of the future prove too much for his limited powers. To gain equal renown, the poet loses renown and the bays go to heaven. The ancients, in the story of Homer and Hesiod's competition, knew that the gods were the judges of poetry; Milton adds that they are also the source. As a result, his poem is a poem of praise for the justness of God's ways as well as an explanation of those ways to man. The bard is no longer singing at the hearth facing us but he has turned his back from man and his face toward heaven. His invocations are now prayers and his story is a series of glosses upon a sacred text, but beneath these rites is a transformed pagan litany that has been returned to its true source. The pagan world has not been destroyed but it has been extended and fulfilled.

Appendix

Throughout this book, I have emphasized the value that Milton placed upon the classical epic. That Milton saw in Homer and Virgil a model for poetic imitation hardly needs any demonstration, but for the discussion above, it will be necessary to keep in mind that Milton saw the classical epic as an important source of theological and philosophical wisdom. In order to treat this neglected aspect of Milton's thought,[1] I wish to examine briefly some of his prose passages that reveal how and why he read the classical epic. Afterward I shall briefly consider his reservations expressed in *Paradise Regained.*

Milton's philosophical and theological *raison d'être* for reverting to classical wisdom appears in *The Christian Doctrine*:[2]

> However, it cannot be denied that some traces of the divine image still remain in us, which are not wholly extinguished by this spiritual death. This is quite clear . . . from the holiness and wisdom in both word and deed of many of the heathens (VI, 396).

In his political controversies, personal letters, and theological discourses, Milton makes great use of classical precept and example. Even when we discount the heat of rhetorical enthusiasm, Milton finds the classical epics illuminating on every subject, even moral philosophy and theology. In the first *Defence of the English People*, Milton finds Virgil, for instance, to have set patterns for correct political behavior in his *Aeneid*:

> in the eighth book of his *Aeneid* Virgil, who was unsurpassed in the creation of what was appropriate, meant with this tale to show Caesar Octavian, even then Rome's ruler, what had been the rights of kings from immemorial ages among all nations (IV, 445).

Milton then quotes *Aen*. VIII, 489–95.

Milton's use of political wisdom from the epic poets is common throughout the first *Defence*. So is Milton's moralizing upon the classical epics, as in *The Reason of Church Government* where Milton cites shame as an incentive to virtue:

> Hence we may read in the *Iliad* where *Hector* being wisht to retire from the battel, many of his forces being routed, makes answer that he durst not for shame, lest the Trojan Knights and Dames should think he did ignobly (I, 840–1; cf. *Il*. VI, 440–6 and XXII, 100).

The same authorities turn up in *The Christian Doctrine* often uniting the pagan and Christian worlds:

> This womanly modesty was found even among the heathen: Homer says of Penelope in *Odyssey* I (333): *στῆ ῥα παρὰ σταθμὸν· τέγεος πύκα ποιητοῖο* 'She stood by the threshold' (VI, 728).

In *The Doctrine and Discipline of Divorce*, Milton finds his way out of the theological dilemma of man's free will by pointing to Homer's epics which demonstrate it:[3]

> mans own freewill self corrupted is the adequat and sufficient cause of his disobedience *besides Fate*; as *Homer* also wanted not to expresse both in his *Iliad* and *Odyssei* (II, 294).

Homer also provides theological proof that man is to blame for his actions, not God. God is assumed to be one with Jupiter; those who think God to blame for hardening men's hearts are told in *The Christian Doctrine* that they:

> do, in fact, accuse God, however strongly they may deny it. Even a heathen like Homer emphatically reproves such people in *Odyssey*, I, 7: 'They perisht by their owne impieties' – and again through the mouth of Jupiter, I, 32:
>
> O how falsely men
> Accuse us Gods as authors of their ill,
> When by the bane their owne bad lives instill
> They suffer all the miseries of their states
> Past our afflictions and beyond their fates (VI, 202).

By referring to Virgil, Milton also justifies expiatory punishments:

> This feature of divine justice, the insistence upon propitiatory sacrifices for sin, was well known among other nations, and never thought to be unfair . . . Virgil *Aeneid*, I, [39–41]:

> *Could angry Pallas with revengeful spleen,*
> *The Grecian navy burn, and drown the men?*
> *She for the fault of one offending foe* . . . (VI, 387).

Milton felt that these and other classical sources must be read as independently and as thoughtfully as the Bible. Far from accepting or denying whatever the ancients said, Milton believed only what he examined in the light of reason and previous knowledge: the classical poets must pass a stiff moral and theological examination from the poet:

> if I found those authors any where speaking unworthy things of themselves; or unchaste of those names which before they had extoll'd, this effect it wrought with me, from that time forward their art I still applauded, but the men I deplor'd (*An Apology Against a Pamphlet*, I, 890).

As he had said earlier in the first *Prolusion*: I 'am only attempting to bring them to the test of reason, and thereby to examine whether they can bear the scrutiny of strict truth' (*Prose*, I, 224). Milton tries to extract the nectar of the ancients but not without constantly correcting pagan error with biblical truth:

> For all antiquity that adds or varies from the Scripture, is no more warranted to our safe imitation, then what was don the Age before at *Trent* (III, 464).

Given these restrictions, the ancients are safe to imitate, as long as the imitator improves what he borrows; so Milton twits the king for 'plagiarizing' one of David's psalms:

> He borrows *Davids* Psalmes, as he charges the *Assembly of Divines* in his twentieth Discourse, *To have set forth old Catechisms and Confessions of faith new drest*. Had he borrow'd *Davids* heart, it had bin much the holier theft. For such kind of borrowing as this, if it be not better'd by the borrower, among good Authors is accounted *Plagiarie* (III, 547).

This admiration for classical wisdom seems slighted in *Paradise Regained*.[4] Without pretending to resolve the controversy, I think we can see that the wisdom of the ancient epic poets is not totally rejected. Milton's last poem was not only almost free of the strong classical influence that is evident in the rest of his poetry, it presents the Renaissance case against the classics: they are the product of ignorance. When Satan tempts the Son with the kingdom of Athens, the philosophical wisdom of Greece, the Son vehemently rejects the offer:[5]

> Who therefore seeks in these
> True wisdom finds her not, or by delusion
> Far worse, her false resemblance only meets,
> An empty cloud (IV, 318–21).

Besides the classical philosophers, the poets in general are inferior to the writers of the Bible, because the classical world derived its arts from the Hebraic world:

> All our Law and Story strew'd
> With Hymns, our Psalms with artful terms inscrib'd
> Our Hebrew Songs and Harps in *Babylon*,
> That pleas'd so well our Victors' ear, declare
> That rather *Greece* from us these arts deriv'd (IV, 334–8).

Though this statement places the classics below the Bible, it does not contradict Milton's earlier writings. He would not have doubted the superiority of the Word of God nor that classical art and wisdom were derived from it. To show how the classics lead back to the Bible is one of the functions of *Paradise Lost*, a route that is clear to the Son of God but not to the sons of men. Yet even the Son adds that the classical poets contain wisdom: 'where moral virtue is express'd/ By light of Nature, not in all quite lost' (IV, 351–2). Here we must place Homer and Virgil.

Notes

Introduction

1 For the commentaries on the classical epics available to, and used by, Milton, see Don Cameron Allen, *Mysteriously Meant: The Rediscovery of Pagan Symbolism and Allegorical Interpretation in the Renaissance*. For the various traditions in interpreting the classics, see Jean Seznec, *The Survival of the Pagan Gods*, tr. Barbara F. Sessions. See also Harris Francis Fletcher, *The Intellectual Development of John Milton* (Urbana: University of Illinois Press, 2 vols, 1956 and 1961). Fletcher has also argued ('Milton's Homer,' *Journal of English and Germanic Philology*, XXXVIII (1939), 229–32) that any work done on Milton and Homer must take into consideration the commentaries of Eustathius, Spondanus, and Junius. His argument was based upon the use of these commentaries in Milton's notes to his copy of Pindar. However, Maurice Kelley and Samuel D. Atkins have seriously challenged the handwriting as Milton's ('Milton and the Harvard Pindar,' *Studies in Bibliography*, XVII (1964), 77–82). The controversy has no effect on my argument, since I am dealing with recognizable parallels between the four epics. Nor are there any textual difficulties that would affect it.

2 The parallels between *Paradise Lost* and the classical epic were first pointed out in *The Poetical Works of Mr. John Milton* (London: J. Tonson, 1695) by the annotations of Patrick Hume. The commentaries only list and do not discuss the classical parallels. Subsequent editions emphasizing the classics are Thomas Newton's *Paradise Lost* (1749); rpt in *The Complete Poems of John Milton*, ed. Thomas Newton (New York: Crown, 1936). Much of this early work went into H. J. Todd's variorum edition *The Poetical Works of John Milton* (1809; rpt New York: AMS Press, 7 vols, 1970). Of the modern editions emphasizing the classics, I have found the following useful: that of A. W. Verity, *Paradise Lost* (Cambridge University Press, 1921); of Merritt Y. Hughes in *John Milton: Complete Poems and Major Prose* (New York: Odyssey Press, 1957); of Douglas Bush in *John Milton: Poetical Works* (Oxford University Press, 1966); and of Alastair Fowler in *The Poems of John Milton*, ed. John Carey and Alastair Fowler (London: Longmans, 1968).

Discussion of Milton's use of classical sources begins with Joseph Addison's 'Critique of *Paradise Lost*,' *Spectator*, 31 December–3 May 1712 (eighteen papers). These essays were conveniently assembled by Albert S. Cook in his *Addison's Criticisms of 'Paradise Lost'* (Boston: Ginn, 1892). These essays are essential to any study of the classical sources of *Paradise Lost* and were continued into *An Essay Upon Milton's Imitations of the Ancients in his 'Paradise Lost'* (London: J. Roberts, 1741), a useful essay by an unknown author.

For a list of later studies, see the Bibliography.

3 Among the proponents of this view are James A. Freeman, 'The Roof was Fretted Gold,' *Comparative Literature*, XXVIII (1975), 265; Sanford Budick, *Poetry of Civilization: Mythopoetic Displacement in the Verse of Milton, Dryden, and Johnson*, p. 61; A.S.P. Woodhouse, *The Heavenly Muse*, ed. Hugh MacCallum, p. 189; Don Cameron Allen, op. cit., p. 293; John Steadman, *Milton and the Renaissance Hero*, p. 1; and C. M. Bowra, *From Virgil to Milton*, p. 228. Cf. *An Essay Upon Milton's Imitations of the Ancients . . .*, pp. 20–1.

These critics are quite right to point out Satan's classicism and the Father's Christianity, but I think there is a subtler blend of these elements in each of these figures rather than a sharp dichotomy. In a word, the 'antithesis' needs further refinement.

4 What Milton found philosophically and theologically valuable in the classical epic is evident in his prose. For a discussion of this point and of the problem of Milton's 'rejection' of the classics in *Paradise Regained*, see the Appendix.

Chapter 1 'Pellax Ulixes': the revaluation of the epic villain

1 All quotations from Milton's poetry are from *John Milton: Complete Poems and Major Prose*, ed. Merritt Y. Hughes (New York: Odyssey Press, 1957).

2 All quotations from Virgil are from *P. Vergili Maronis Opera*, ed. R.A.B. Mynors (Oxford: Clarendon Press, 1969). The translations are mine. B. A. Wright's comment appears in 'Note on *Paradise Lost*, II, 70–81,' *Notes and Queries*, new series, V (1958), 208–9.

3 Cf. I, 123; II, 17, 197, 232, 393, 550, 559, 560, 610.

4 A history of this well-known simile is given in Bowra, *From Virgil to Milton*, pp. 240–1. Cf. also James P. Holoka, 'Thick as Autumnal Leaves,' *Milton Quarterly*, X (1976), 78–83.

5 Harding rightly points out the traditional association between the gigantomachia and the fall of the angels: *The Club of Hercules*, pp. 57–9. Newton, who cites the parallel, also reminds us of *Il.* VIII, 16, where Zeus says that Tartaros is as far below Hades as heaven is above it. Epic emulation drove Virgil to double the

distance involved and Milton to triple it. Cf. Katherine Lever, 'Milton and Homer, the Monarchs of the Mount,' *Bucknell Review*, XII (1964), 57–64.

6 The source is found in Newton. This scene reminds John E. Seaman, in 'Homeric Parody at the Gates of Milton's Hell,' *Modern Language Review*, LXII (1967), 212–13, of *Il*. VI, 119–236, the encounter of Glaukos and Diomedes.

7 This simile of the bees is analyzed by Harding, op. cit., pp. 103–8.

8 Ibid., p. 108; Addison, *Spectator*, 333.

9 For a discussion of this belief, see Seznec, *The Survival of the Pagan Gods*, p. 17.

10 *Spectator*, 333.

11 Biblical weapons are discussed by J. R. Lumby in *A Companion to Biblical Studies*, ed. W. Emery Barnes (Cambridge University Press, 1916), pp. 380–2.

12 Steadman notes (*Milton and the Renaissance Hero*, p. 9) that Achilles was viewed as a positive example by most Renaissance writers. Milton uses him as a foil to show off the villainy of Satan's heroism. This technique is the same one Virgil used when he made Turnus into an Achilles gone wrong. Hence the parallels between Satan and Turnus that Robert M. Boltwood sees in 'Turnus and Satan as Epic Villains,' *Classical Journal*, XLVII (1952), 183–6. Cf. Mario A. DiCesare, '*Paradise Lost* and Epic Tradition,' *Milton Studies*, I (1969), 31–50. I think that what is most important is the figure of Achilles in the background.

13 Cf. Achilles' prayers, XVI, 228–48.

14 All quotations from Homer are from *Homeri Opera*, ed. David B. Monroe and Thomas W. Allen, 3rd edn (Oxford: Clarendon Press, 5 vols, 1911–20). The translations are mine.

15 E.g., the boasts of Sarpedon, V, 472–92 and Hector, XVI, 830–42, the 'hybris' of which prefigures their deaths. Cf. in the *Aeneid*, the boasting and death of Pandarus, IX, 737–9 and Liger, X, 581–3.

16 Satan's Odyssean methods in general form the subject of John M. Steadman's 'The Classical Hero: Satan and Ulysses,' *Milton's Epic Characters: Image and Idol*, pp. 194–208. Cf. Manoocher Aryanpur, '*Paradise Lost* and the *Odyssey*,' *Texas Studies in Language and Literature*, IX (1967), 151–66.

17 See W. B. Stanford, *The Ulysses Theme*, 2nd edn (Ann Arbor: University of Michigan Press, 1968).

18 Steadman, 'The Classical Hero: Satan and Ulysses,' pp. 194–208.

19 On Milton's shying away from allegory in his epic, see Steadman, *Milton and the Renaissance Hero*, pp. 178–84, and Ann Gossman, 'Maia's Son: Milton and the Renaissance Virgil,' *Studies in*

Medieval, Renaissance, [and] American Literature: a Festschrift, ed. Betsy F. Colquitt, pp. 109–19.

20 In his *History of the World* (1614), Sir Walter Raleigh calculated that 1,917 years elapsed between the death of Adam and the fall of Troy. His tables appear at the end of the 11th edn (London: C. Conyers *et al.*, 2 vols, 1736) [no pagination].

Chapter 2 Above the Olympian Mount

1 Abdiel is a good example of how the epic tradition can supply a context for a Christian character in Milton. As Mason Tung and others have shown, Abdiel's behavior is narrated by Raphael in order to exemplify to Adam the free will, moral courage, and right reason that men as well as angels can rely upon in the hour of temptation. See Tung's 'The Abdiel Episode: A Contextual Reading,' *Studies in Philology*, LXII (1965), 595–609; John S. Diekhof, *Milton's 'Paradise Lost': A Commentary on the Argument* (1946; rpt New York: Humanities Press, 1968), pp. 87–9; and Douglas Knight, 'The Dramatic Center of *Paradise Lost*,' *Southern Atlantic Quarterly*, LXIII (1964), 44–59. For the structural significance of Abdiel, see Joseph H. Summers, *The Muse's Method* (1962; rpt New York: Norton, 1968), pp. 112–13, 123–7. But two aspects of Abdiel have remained problematic: why did Milton assign such a role to an obscure angel and why did only Abdiel oppose Satan? Michael, Gabriel, Raphael, and Uriel, being well known from biblical literature, seem more likely opponents of Satan. Vondel, for instance, in his *Lucifer* (translated and anthologized by Watson Kirkconnell in *The Celestial Cycle* (University of Toronto Press, 1952)) used both Michael and Raphael to argue with Satan, while Milton's angel appears only in a catalogue in the *Book of Raziel*: see Grant McColley, *'Paradise Lost': An Account of Its Growth and Major Origins* (1940; rpt New York: Russell & Russell, 1963), pp. 34–7; Allan H. Gilbert, *On the Composition of 'Paradise Lost'* (1947; rpt New York: Octagon, 1966), pp. 123–7 and Robert H. West, *Milton and the Angels* (Athens, Georgia: University of Georgia Press, 1955), pp. 124, 134, and 152–4. George H. Whiting's suggestion that Abdiel has a parallel in Abdias ('Abdiel and the Prophet Abdias,' *Studies in Philology*, LX (1963), 214–26) and Jack Goldman's suggestive biblical parallels to Noah, Phineas, and Elijah ('Insight into Milton's Abdiel,' *Philological Quarterly*, XLIX (1970), 249–54) do not explain why Milton relegated such a role to an obscure angel, unless it was the etymology of the name that appealed to him; Abdiel means 'servant of God,' but then so does Abdias. Goldman further points out that Abdiel also can mean 'I will secede'

(p. 252), but Milton does not often introduce characters whose names only have significance, so I think the obscurity is important in itself and has the classical roots explained above.

The classical context also explains the solitariness of Abdiel's behavior, since by convention, the epic malcontent then can help answer the objections of David Daiches, 'What was Abdiel doing among Satan's forces anyway?' (*Milton* (1959; rpt New York, 1966), pp. 197–8); of A. J. A. Waldock, who finds Abdiel merely 'Milton's mouthpiece,' who is really bested by Satan in the argument (*'Paradise Lost' and its Critics* (Cambridge University Press, 1947), p. 71); and of John Peter, who finds the scene 'absurd,' because it is implausible, 'controlled and confirmed neither by the Bible nor any other external authority' (*A Critique of 'Paradise Lost'* (New York: Columbia University Press, 1960), p. 71, see esp. pp. 69–73). The classical background extends Abdiel's significance beyond the biographical explanations that have been offered: that Milton saw Abdiel and himself as the one just man in a corrupt society, a view that Milton had taken after the Revolution had failed. See A. W. Verity, *Paradise Lost* (Cambridge University Press, 1921), p. 508; James Holly Hanford, *John Milton: Englishman* (New York: Crown, 1949), pp. 197–8; and Émile Saillens, *John Milton: Man-Poet-Polemist* (Oxford: Basil Blackwell, 1964), p. 284. John Steadman (*Milton and the Renaissance Hero*, pp. xvi, 66, and 145) has pointed out that Abdiel has some of the qualities of an epic hero, such as wisdom, fortitude, 'amor,' and especially zeal, but he does not relate him to any specific epic convention. Steadman answers Waldock's charge that Satan defeats Abdiel in their argument (see *Milton's Epic Characters*, pp. 163–6). Abdiel's appearance, it should be added, caused no difficulty to two earlier readers of Milton who viewed his epic from a classical standpoint: Samuel Johnson (*Lives of the English Poets*, ed. George Birbeck Hill (Oxford: Clarendon Press, 1905), vol. III, p. 204) and Addison (*Spectator*, 327). Manoocher Aryanpur (*'Paradise Lost* and the *Odyssey*,' *Texas Studies in Language and Literature*, IX (1967), 164) has seen a parallel between Abdiel and another epic malcontent, Eurylokos. Other, more imperfect, parallels besides Eurylokos (*Od.* X, 251–74) are Theoklymenos (*Od.* XX, 364–70), Halitherses (*Od.* XXIV, 451–62), Pyrgo (*Aen.* V, 644–52), Laocoön (*Aen.* II, 201–31), and Drances (*Aen.* XI, 336–444). All these obscure figures oppose some heroic action and are overruled.

2 E.g. by Hector, III, 39–57; by Menelaos, III, 97–102; by Helen, VI, 344–8; by Antenor, VII, 350–3; and by Achilles, IX, 337–9.

3 Harding, *The Club of Hercules*, pp. 101–3; Thomas M. Greene, *The Descent from Heaven*, pp. 363–418. Greene also discusses the descent convention in general. A fourth source, Aeneas' visit to

Evander, has been suggested by John R. Knott, Jr in 'The Visit of Raphael: *Paradise Lost*, Book V,' *Philological Quarterly*, XLVII (1968), 36–42, but this echo is less distinct than the other three, and the earlier Virgilian echo predominates. Milton's scene is more *retractatio* than *contaminatio*.

4 Here the classical source is more important than the biblical. The major biblical source is the visit of the three angels to Abraham (Gen. XVIII): both Abraham and Adam are in the doorway when the celestial messenger arrives, both instruct their wives to prepare the best food, both hear of their future offspring, both learn of judgments to come (Adam learns of the Last Judgment and Abraham learns of the judgment on Sodom and Gomorrah), and both speak to their celestial visitors (pointed out by James H. Sims in *The Bible in Milton's Epics* (Gainsville: University of Florida Press, 1962), pp. 201–4). Cf. Harold Fisch, 'Hebraic Style and Motifs in *Paradise Lost*,' in *Language and Style in Milton*, ed. Ronald David Emma and John Shawcrosse (New York: Frederick Ungar, 1967), pp. 53–6, and Jason P. Rosenblatt, 'Celestial Entertainment in Eden: Book V of *Paradise Lost*,' *Harvard Theological Review*, LXII (1969), 411–27.

5 The phrase but not the convention originates in *Od.* XIV, 435 ('*Μαιάδος υἱεῖ*') and is a common epithet for Hermes in the Homeric Hymn, 'To Hermes.' Cf. Hesiod, *The Homeric Hymns, and Homerica*, ed. and tr. Hugh G. Evelyn-White (Cambridge, Mass.: Harvard University Press, 1947), pp. 362–405.

6 For the phoenix as symbol of Christ, see George Ferguson, *Signs and Symbols in Christian Art* (1954; rpt New York: Oxford University Press, 1966), p. 23.

7 The Latin text appears in *The Works of John Milton*, ed. Frank Allen Patterson (New York: Columbia University Press, 1931–8), XV, 182.

8 J. A. K. Thomson, *Classical Influences on English Poetry*, p. 58. As Arnold Williams has shown, in *The Common Expositor*, pp. 199–215, biblical commentators frequently resorted to the classics to show the erroneous transmission of the ideas of Moses.

9 In Page's edition of the *Aeneid* (London: Macmillan, 1894), I, 205.

10 As editors often note (e.g. Hughes), there is an allusion here also to the gigantomachia of Hesiod (*Theogony*, 713–20) where the giants too throw mountains. J. A. K. Thomson has pointed to the connection between the mountains of the angels and the stones of heroes (op. cit., p. 58).

11 For the Son as epic hero, see Steadman, *Milton and the Renaissance Hero*, *passim*, and John E. Seaman, 'The Chivalric Cast of Milton's Hero,' *English Studies*, XLIX (1968), 97–107.

12 The controversy over Milton's God is summed up by Sister M. Hilda Bonham in 'Milton's Ways with God,' dissertation,

University of Michigan, 1964. Aside from casual comments (e.g., C. S. Lewis, *A Preface to 'Paradise Lost,'* p. 127; Douglas Bush, 'Virgil and Milton,' *Classical Journal*, XLVII (1952), 179; John M. Steadman, 'The God of *Paradise Lost* and the *Divina Commedia*,' *Archiv für das Studium der Neuren Sprachen und Literaturen*, CXCV (1959), 273–89; and Joan Webber, 'Milton's God,' *English Literary History*, XL (1973), 514–31, esp. 526), the Father has not been examined as part of the epic tradition, though a start was made by Willard Connely, in 'Imprints of the *Aeneid* on *Paradise Lost*,' *Classical Journal*, XVIII (1923), 466–76, who finds God colorless beside Jupiter.

13 A comparison between Milton and Michelangelo is the subject of Alexander S. Twombly's *The Masterpieces of Michelangelo and Milton* (Boston: Silver, Burdett, 1896).

14 On the confusion of fate and the will of the gods, see Martin P. Nilsson, *A History of Greek Religion*, 2nd edn, tr. F. J. Fielden (1949; rpt New York: Norton, 1964), pp. 167–72. Cf. the article on 'fate' in *The Oxford Classical Dictionary*, ed. N. G. L. Hammond and H. H. Scullard, 2nd edn (Oxford: Clarendon Press, 1970).

15 A tradition stemming from Homer and continuing into the Renaissance made this chain the emblem of universal harmony. See Fowler's comments on Milton's passage: *The Poems of John Milton*, ed. John Carey and Alastair Fowler (London: Longmans, 1968), pp. 557–8.

16 *Essays of John Dryden*, ed. W. P. Ker (Oxford University Press, 1900), vol. II, pp. 212–13. Dryden also pointed out the biblical allusion to the Book of Daniel (V: 27): 'you have been weighed in the balances and found wanting,' the prophet's words to Belshazzar and a good merging of the Christian and pagan motifs in *Paradise Lost.* Virgilian parallels are pressed by A. S. Ferguson in '*Paradise Lost*, IV, 977–1015,' *Modern Language Review*, XV (1920), 168–70.

17 The wrath of God is, of course, a familiar biblical theme, e.g., Milton's translation of the second Psalm where the Lord reacts against His enemies: 'the Lord shall scoff them, then severe/ Speak to them in his wrath, and in his fell/ And fierce ire trouble them' (ll. 9–11). Like many aspects of Milton's theology in *Paradise Lost*, Milton uses common ground between classical and pagan. In this case, he resorts to one of the less popular traditions of the Renaissance. Cf. C. A. Patrides, *Milton and the Christian Tradition* (Oxford University Press, 1966), p. 156.

18 See the Appendix.

19 Northrop Frye, *The Return of Eden* (University of Toronto Press, 1965), p. 99.

Chapter 3 'Et in Arcadia Ego': the conflict in Eden

1 By J. A. K. Thomson (*Classical Influences on English Poetry*, p. 21) and A. S. P. Woodhouse (*The Heavenly Muse*, p. 197).

2 For Eve and Dido: see Connely, 'Imprints of the *Aeneid* on *Paradise Lost*,' *Classical Journal*, XVIII (1923), 469; Harding, *The Club of Hercules*, pp. 88–9; Woodhouse, op. cit., p. 199. Eve's resemblance to Circe is discussed by Leonora Leet Brodwin in 'Milton and the Renaissance Circe,' *Milton Studies*, VI (1974), 21–83 and by S. A. Demetrakopolous in 'Eve as a Circean and Courtly Fatal Woman,' *Milton Quarterly*, IX (1975), 99–107.

3 Criticisms of Milton's attitude towards women are discussed by Barbara K. Lewalski in 'Milton on Women – Yet Once More,' *Milton Studies*, VI (1974), 3–20.

4 A non-epic source is Catullus 11. 22–3.

5 See Tasso's *Discorsi del Poema Erotico* in *Torquato Tasso: Prose*, ed. Ettore Mazzali (Milan: Riccardo Ricciardi, n.d.), p. 549.

6 *Poetics*, 1462b. *Aristotle's Theory of Poetry and Fine Art*, ed. and trans. S. H. Butcher, 2nd edn (London, 1898), p. 110.

7 Martin Mueller, '*Paradise Lost* and the *Iliad*,' *Comparative Literature Studies*, VI (1969), 292–316.

8 Ibid., 302.

9 This extremely relevant source has been surprisingly neglected by all the major commentaries except that of Douglas Bush.

10 'Gods' primarily refers to Gen. III: 4–5: 'Then the serpent said to the woman, Ye shall not dye at all, but God doeth knowe, that when ye shal eat thereof, your eyes shalbe opened, & ye shalbe as gods' (The Geneva Bible: A Facsimile of the 1560 edition (Madison, Milwaukee, and London: University of Wisconsin Press, 1969)). The Oxford Bible emends to 'God,' but the Renaissance edition preserves the ambiguity.

11 Erwin Panofsky analyzed this tradition in art: '*Et in Arcadia Ego*: Poussin and the Elegaic Tradition,' *Meaning in the Visual Arts* (Garden City, NJ: Doubleday, 1955), pp. 295–320.

12 Hughes cites *Il.* XIV, 83. Cf. also *Il.* IV, 350 and *Od.* I, 64; III, 230; V, 22; XIX, 492; XXI, 168; XXIII, 70.

13 *Spectator*, 351.

14 Thomson, op. cit., p. 61. As John E. Seaman points out ('The Epic Art of *Paradise Lost*: A Study of Milton's Use of Epic Conventions,' dissertation, Stanford, 1962, p. 225), the fall of man and the fall of Troy were conflated in the Middle Ages but not in Renaissance England, since the English viewed Troy as a fact of history and traced their own national ancestry from it. The idea of Eve as the destroyer of Troy and paradise is found in Henry Reynolds, however:

> What can *Homers Ate*, whom he calls the first daughter of *Iupiter*, and

poem. Cf. Douglas Knight, 'The Dramatic Center of *Paradise Lost*,' *Southern Atlantic Quarterly*, LXIII (1964), 44–59.

5 The basic book on Milton's style is Christopher Ricks' *Milton's Grand Style*. Ricks does not investigate classical elements in any detail, however, so for the 'Virgilianism' of Milton's style, turn to Addison, *Spectator*, 285, Bowra (*From Virgil to Milton*, p. 198), Thomson (*Classical Influences on English Poetry*, pp. 61–71), Tillyard, 'Milton and the Classics' (in *Essays by Divers Hands*, pp. 60–3), Henry Rushton Fairclough, 'The Influence of Virgil Upon the Forms of English Verse,' *Classical Journal*, XXVI (1930), 74–94. See also K. W. Gransden, '*Paradise Lost* and the *Aeneid*,' *Essays in Criticism*, XVII (1967), 281–303; Mario DiCesare, 'Adventurous Song: The Texture of Milton's Epic,' in *Language and Style in Milton*, ed. Ronald David Emma and John T. Shawcrosse, pp. 1–29; Donald R. Pearce, 'The Style of Milton's Epic,' in *Milton: Modern Essays in Criticism*, ed. Arthur E. Barker, pp. 368–85; and Janette Richardson, 'Virgil and Milton once again,' *Comparative Literature*, XIV (1962), 321–31.

6 Aristotle, *Poetics*, 1458ª–1459ᵇ.

7 Or even smaller units considering the use of formulae. A convenient discussion of the Homeric formulae is given by C. M. Bowra in *A Companion to Homer*, ed. Alan J. B. Wace and Frank H. Stubbings (New York: Macmillan, 1963), pp. 26–37. The standard source is *The Making of Homeric Verse: The Collected Papers of Milman Parry*, ed. Adam Parry (Oxford University Press, 1971).

8 Virgil's use of sibilant sounds is pointed out by R. G. Austin in his edition of the second book of the *Aeneid*, *Aeneidos: Liber Secundus* (Oxford: Clarendon Press, 1964), p. 103.

9 This word occurs eighteen times in the *Aeneid*: I, 314; III, 499; VI, 880; VIII, 111; IX, 56; X, 328, 380, 552, 662, 694, 734, 770, 877; XI, 498, 504; XII, 298, 481, 540. For Virgil's use of 'labor,' cf. *Aen.* I, 77; II, 708; III, 714; IV, 379.

10 Other instances are I, 91; II, 995; VI, 193, 456, 519, 670, 797, 874; IX, 275, 493. For Virgil's use of 'ruo' cf. also *Aen.* II, 290, 363; IX, 438, 516, 695.

11 For Landor's comment, see *The Complete Works of Walter Savage Landor*, ed. T. Earle Welby (London: Chapman & Hall, 1927–36), vol. V, p. 258.

12 *Chapman's Homer*, ed. Allardyce Nicoll, 2nd edn (Princeton University Press, 1967).

13 For the Renaissance concept of glory as the goal of true and false heroic virtue, see John M. Steadman, *Milton and the Renaissance Hero*, pp. 14, 142–4, and 195–200. It is a key term in *The Fairie Queene* where Spenser wishes to be inspired by Queen Elizabeth's 'true glorious type' (I, 4) (*Spenser: Poetical Works*, ed. J. C. Smith and E. De Selincourt (London: Oxford University Press, 1912)).

Herbert makes the contrast when he tells of the progress of sin:

> From *Greece* he went to *Rome*; and as before
> He was a God, now he's an Emperour.
> *Nero* and others lodg'd him bravely there,
> Put him in trust to rule the Roman sphere.
> Glorie was his chief instrument of old.

Cf. *Paradise Lost* (VI, 289–90) ('The Church Militant,' *Works*, p. 194). Herbert begins his 'L'Envoy,' which follows 'The Church Militant,' with *'King of Glorie'* (p. 199), an address to the true source and exemplification of glory.

14 The basic work on the Miltonic simile has been done by James Whaler: 'The Miltonic Simile,' *Publications of the Modern Language Association of America*, XLVI (1931), 1034–74; 'Grammatical Nexus of the Miltonic Simile,' *Journal of English and Germanic Philology*, XXX (1931), 327–34; 'Compounding and Distribution of Similes in *Paradise Lost*,' *Modern Philology*, XXVIII (1931), 313–34; 'Animal Simile in *Paradise Lost*,' *Publications of the Modern Language Association of America*, XLVII (1932), 534–53; *Counterpoint and Symbol: An Inquiry into the Rhythm of Milton's Epic Simile*. Whaler finds in Milton a more organic use of similes than in the earlier epic poets and a conscious emulation of Virgil and Homer. See also Addison, *Spectator*, 303; John S. Coolidge, 'Great Things and Small: The Virgilian Progression,' *Comparative Literature*, XVII (1965), 1–23; Knight, op. cit.; Kingsley Widmer, 'The Iconography of Renunciation: The Miltonic Simile,' in *Milton's Epic Poetry*, ed. C. A. Patrides, pp. 121–31; Ricks, op. cit., pp. 118–50; Warren D. Anderson, 'Notes on the Simile in Homer and His Successors: II. Milton,' *Classical Journal*, LIII (1957), 127–33. Some useful remarks on the classical and post-classical simile appear in C. M. Bowra's *Tradition and Design in the 'Iliad'* (Oxford: Clarendon Press, 1930), pp. 114–28.

15 In his commentary on Milton (1732), Richard Bentley wished to delete the words, 'The careful Plowman doubting stands/ Lest on the Threshing floor his hopeful sheaves/ Prove chaff.' Bentley gave as his reason, that, while it is permissible to compare the motion of the angels to a gentle breeze, adding the comparison of a tempest is an 'injury' to the previous simile. Then asking, 'what are sheaves bound up in a Barn to the Phalanx, that hem'd Satan?' and 'where's the least similitude?', Bentley concluded that the second part of the comparison was an editor's fabrication because Milton's Satan could not confound the orderly armies of heaven (*Paradise Lost: A New Edition* (London: Jacob Jonson & John Poulson, 1732), p. 143). William Empson too thought the simile inappropriate, for 'it certainly makes the angels look weak.' Empson added that the reference to the plowman is vague because the identity of the plowman is unclear. If God is the

plowman, claimed Empson, He is clearly not omnipotent because he 'doubting stands'; if Satan is the plowman, he is anxious only for a moment, because 'he is the natural ruler and owner of the good angels.' To Empson, the whole comparison made Satan a grander figure than any of the loyal angels who guard Eden ('Milton and Bentley' in *Some Versions of Pastoral* (London: Chatto & Windus, 1935), pp. 149–91). Christopher Ricks, while not acceding to Empson's interpretation, could not defend the simile on artistic grounds, concluding it was 'beautiful but digressive' (op. cit., p. 130). Alastair Fowler suggested that since threshing is a biblical metaphor for divine judgment, the plowman may be God, who is 'careful that the final judgment, and the final reckoning with Satan, should not be premature' (*The Poems of John Milton* (London: Longmans, 1968), pp. 669–70). R. D. Bedford ('Similes of Unlikeness in *Paradise Lost*,' *Essays in Criticism*, XXV (1975), 179–96) saw the plowman as Adam, Abel, the peasant, and the reader, and C. Schaar ('*Paradise Lost* IV, 977–85 and V, 706–10,' *English Studies*, LXVI (1975), 215–16) saw the plowman as God fearful that the angels would waver in fighting.

16 Charles Rowan Beye points to the domestic and natural world pictured in the Homeric simile, a world with its own violence (*The 'Iliad,' The 'Odyssey,' and the Epic Tradition* (New York: Anchor, 1966), pp. 108–9).

17 Milton's sarcasm does not lessen the magnitude of Satan's army from a human perspective. Milton gets the best out of both sides of the simile: Satan is grand from the earthly and epic viewpoint but puny from the divine perspective.

18 E.g., *Aen.* II, 304–8; 355–8; 379–81; 416–19; 470–5; 496–9. In a sense, of course, everything that Raphael says is one long simile.

19 The basic work on Milton's narrator is Anne Davidson Ferry's *Milton's Epic Voice: The Narrator in 'Paradise Lost'* (Cambridge, Mass.: Harvard University Press, 1967), but Mrs Ferry does not deal with the classical tradition nor does Rodney Delasanta, *The Epic Voice* (The Hague: Mouton, 1967). See also Robert M. Durling, *The Figure of the Poet in Renaissance Epic* (Cambridge, Mass.: Harvard University Press, 1965); Edward L. Herbst, 'Classical Mythology in *Paradise Lost*,' *Classical Philology*, XXIX (1934), 147–8; J. T. Sheppard, *The Pattern of the 'Iliad'* (1922; rpt New York: Barnes & Noble, 1969), pp. 212–13. As the epic poet who put himself most directly into his work and who Christianized the epic address was Dante, the reader may also wish to consult Erich Auerbach, 'Dante's Addresses to the Reader,' in *Parnassus Revisited*, ed. Anthony C. Yu (Chicago: American Library Association, 1973), pp. 121–31.

20 *Poetics*, 1460^{a}.

21 *Spectator*, 327.

22 Since antiquity, theorists have inveighed against this technique, but poets and novelists continue to use it. Aristotle said that the poet should not address the reader in his own voice for he breaks the illusion of imitation (*Poetics*, 1460[a]). In *Spectator*, 297, Addison agrees, but Sir John Harrington (1591) finds that it is a pleasing fault, at least in Ariosto:

> Another fault is that he speaketh so much in his own person by digression which they say also is against the rules of Poetrie because neither *Homer* nor *Virgill* did it. Me thinks it is a sufficient defence to say, *Ariosto* doth it; sure I am, it is both delightfull and verie profitable and an excellent breathing place for the reader, and even as if a man walked in a faire long alley to have a seat or resting place here and there is easie and commodious . . . .

'A Preface, or Rather a Brief Apology of Poetrie,' in *Ludivico Ariosto's 'Orlando Furioso,'* ed. Robert McNulty (Oxford: Clarendon Press, 1972), p. 13.

23 In the *Odyssey*, the peculiar phrase, *'Εὔμαιε συβῶτα,'* 'O swineherd Eumaeus!' appears fourteen times between Books XIV and XVII. It may be an outburst on the part of Homer or a ballad-singer's interpolation. See W. B. Stanford's edition of the *Odyssey*, 2nd edn (London: Macmillan, 1958), II, 218. All the addresses to Patroklos appear in Book XVI (20, 584, 692, 744, 754, 787, 812, 843).

24 Cf. D. C. Allen, 'Milton and the Descent to Light,' *Milton: Modern Essays in Criticism*, ed. Arthur E. Barker, pp. 177–95.

25 Gilbert Murray, *The Classical Tradition in Poetry* (Cambridge, Mass.: Harvard University Press, 1927), pp. 9–10.

26 Or according to another account for maintaining that women received more pleasure out of the sex act than men. Cf. these entries in *The Oxford Classical Dictionary*.

Appendix

1 Don Cameron Allen did notice it in relation to Homer: see *Mysteriously Meant*, p. 295.

2 All quotations from Milton's prose are from *The Complete Prose Works of John Milton*, ed. Don M. Wolfe *et al.* (New Haven: Yale University Press, 1953ff.), to be published in 8 vols. The translations in the Appendix are from this edition.

3 For Homer's expressions of man's free will, cf. *Il.* XII, 243, and *Od*. I, 32–4.

4 Cf. the assessment of the problem by Barbara K. Lewalski in *Milton's Brief Epic: The Genre, Meaning, and Art of 'Paradise Regained,'* pp. 282–302. Cf. also Lawrence A. Sasek, 'Milton's

Criticism of Greek Literature in *Paradise Regained*,' *Essays in Honor of Esmond Linworth Marilla*, ed. Thomas A. Kirby and William J. Olive, pp. 158–65.

5 For the edition of Milton's poetry, see ch. 1, n.1.

Select bibliography of secondary material

(For editions and critical works before 1900, see Introduction, n. 2.)

Allen, Don Cameron, *Mysteriously Meant: The Rediscovery of Pagan Symbolism and Allegorical Interpretation in the Renaissance*, Baltimore: Johns Hopkins Press, 1970.

Anderson, Warren D., 'Notes on the Simile in Homer and his Successors: II. Milton,' *Classical Journal*, LIII (1957), 127–33.

Aryanpur, Manoocher, '*Paradise Lost* and the *Odyssey*,' *Texas Studies in Language and Literature*, IX (1967), 151–66.

Barker, Arthur E., 'Structural Pattern in *Paradise Lost*,' *Milton: Modern Essays in Criticism*, ed. Arthur E. Barker, New York: Oxford University Press, 1965, pp. 142–55.

Boltwood, Robert M., 'Turnus and Satan as Epic Villains,' *Classical Journal*, XLVII (1952), 183–6.

Bowra, C. M., *From Virgil to Milton*, New York: St Martin's, 1945.

Brodwin, Leonora Leet, 'Milton and the Renaissance Circe,' *Milton Studies*, VI (1974), 21–83.

Budick, Sanford, *Poetry of Civilization: Mythopoetic Displacement in the Verse of Milton, Dryden, and Johnson*, New Haven: Yale University Press, 1974.

Buff, Friedrich, *Miltons Verhältnisse zur Aeneide, Ilias, und Odyssee*, Munich: Hof. a.s., 1904.

Bush, Douglas, 'The Isolation of the Renaissance Hero,' *Reason and the Imagination*, ed. J. A. Mazzeo, New York: Columbia University Press, 1962, pp. 57–69.

Bush, Douglas, *Mythology and the Renaissance Tradition in English Poetry*, 2nd edn, New York: Norton, 1963.

Bush, Douglas, 'Notes on Milton's Classical Mythology,' *Studies in Philology*, XXVIII (1931), 259–72.

Bush, Douglas, *Pagan Myth and Christian Tradition in Poetry*, Philadelphia: American Philosophical Society, 1968.

Bush, Douglas, 'Virgil and Milton,' *Classical Journal*, XLVII (1952), 178–82, 203–4.

Collett, Jonathan H., 'Milton's Use of Classical Mythology in *Paradise Lost*,' *Publications of the Modern Language Association of America*, LXXXV (1970), 88–96.

Condee, Ralph W., 'The Formalized Openings of Milton's Epic

Poems,' *Journal of English and Germanic Philology*, L (1951), 502–8.
Connely, Willard, 'Imprints of the *Aeneid* on *Paradise Lost*,' *Classical Journal*, XVIII (1923), 466–76.
DiCesare, Mario A., 'Adventurous Song: The Texture of Milton's Epic,' *Language and Style in Milton*, ed. Ronald David Emma and John T. Shawcrosse, New York: Frederick Ungar, 1967, pp. 1–29.
DiCesare, Mario A., '*Paradise Lost* and Epic Tradition,' *Milton Studies*, I (1969), 31–50.
Fairclough, Henry Rushton, 'The Influence of Virgil Upon the Forms of English Verse,' *Classical Journal*, XXVI (1930), 74–94.
Farrison, W. Edward, 'The Classical Allusions in *Paradise Lost*, Books I and II,' *English Journal*, XXII (1933), 650–3.
Freeman, James A., 'The Roof was Fretted Gold,' *Comparative Literature*, XXVIII (1975), 254–66.
Gossman, Ann, 'Maia's Son: Milton and the Renaissance Virgil,' *Studies in Medieval, Renaissance, [and] American Literature: a Festschrift*, ed. Betsy F. Colquitt, Fort Worth: Texas Christian University Press, 1971, pp. 109–19.
Gransden, K. W., '*Paradise Lost* and the *Aeneid*,' *Essays in Criticism*, XVII (1967), 281–303.
Greene, Thomas M., *The Descent from Heaven*, New Haven: Yale University Press, 1963.
Hammond, Mason, '*Concilia Deorum* from Homer through Milton,' *Studies in Philology*, XXX (1933), 1–16.
Harding, Davis P., *The Club of Hercules: Studies in the Classical Background of 'Paradise Lost,'* Urbana: University of Illinois Press, 1962.
Herbst, Edward L., 'Classical Mythology in *Paradise Lost*,' *Classical Philology*, XXIX (1934), 147–8.
Huoka, James P., 'Thick as Autumnal Leaves,' *Milton Quarterly*, X (1976), 78–83.
Knight, Douglas, 'The Dramatic Center of *Paradise Lost*,' *Southern Atlantic Quarterly*, LXIII (1964), 44–59.
Lever, Katherine, 'Classical Scholars and Anglo-Classic Poets,' *Classical Journal*, LXIV (1969), 216–18.
Lever, Katherine, 'Milton and Homer, the Monarchs of the Mount,' *Bucknell Review*, XII (1964), 57–64.
Lewalski, Barbara K., *Milton's Brief Epic: The Genre, Meaning, and Art of 'Paradise Regained,'* Providence: Brown University Press, 1966.
Lewis, C. S., *A Preface to 'Paradise Lost,'* London: Oxford University Press, 1942.
Mackail, J. W., *The Springs of Helicon*, London: Longmans, 1909.
McKeon, Richard, 'Literary Criticism and the Concept of Imitation in Antiquity,' *Modern Philology*, XXXIV (1936), 1–35.
Mueller, Martin, '*Paradise Lost* and the *Iliad*,' *Comparative Literature Studies*, VI (1969), 292–316.

Mueller, Martin, 'The Tragic Epic: *Paradise Lost* and the *Iliad*,' dissertation, Indiana, 1966.

Murray, Gilbert, *The Classical Tradition in Poetry*, Cambridge, Mass.: Harvard University Press, 1927.

Nitchie, Elizabeth, *Vergil and the English Poets*, New York: Columbia University Press, 1919.

Osgood, Charles Grosvenor, *The Classical Mythology of Milton's English Poems*, 1900; rpt New York: Gordian Press, 1963.

Pearce, Donald R., 'The Style of Milton's Epic,' *Milton: Modern Essays in Criticism*, ed. Arthur E. Barker, New York: Oxford University Press, 1965, pp. 368–85.

Richardson, Janette, 'Virgil and Milton once again,' *Comparative Literature*, XIV (1962), 321–31.

Ricks, Christopher, *Milton's Grand Style*, Oxford: Clarendon Press, 1963.

Riley, Edgar H., 'Milton's Tribute to Virgil,' *Studies in Philology*, XXVI (1929), 155–65.

Sasek, Lawrence A., 'Milton's Criticism of Greek Literature in *Paradise Regained*,' *Essays in Honor of Esmond Linworth Marilla*, ed. Thomas A. Kirby and William J. Olive, Baton Rouge: Louisiana State University Press, 1970, pp. 158–65.

Sasek, Lawrence A., 'Satan and the Epic Hero,' dissertation, Harvard, 1953.

Seaman, John E., 'The Chivalric Cast of Milton's Hero,' *English Studies*, XLIX (1968), 97–107.

Seaman, John E., 'The Epic Art of *Paradise Lost*: A Study of Milton's Use of Epic Conventions,' dissertation, Stanford, 1962.

Seaman, John E., 'Homeric Parody at the Gates of Milton's Hell,' *Modern Language Review*, LXII (1967), 212–13.

Seaman, John E., *The Moral Paradox of 'Paradise Lost,'* The Hague: Mouton, 1971.

Seznec, Jean, *The Survival of the Pagan Gods*, tr. Barbara F. Sessions, Princeton University Press, 1953.

Smith, Hallett, *Elizabethan Poetry*, Cambridge, Mass.: Harvard University Press, 1952.

Spaeth, J. Duncan, 'Epic Conventions in *Paradise Lost*,' *Elizabethan Studies in Honor of George F. Reynolds*, Boulder: University of Colorado, 1945, pp. 201–10.

Spencer, T. J. B., '*Paradise Lost*: The Anti-Epic,' *Approaches to 'Paradise Lost,'* ed. C. A. Patrides, University of Toronto Press, 1968, pp. 81–98.

Steadman, John M., 'The Classical Hero: Satan and Ulysses,' *Milton's Epic Characters: Image and Idol*, Chapel Hill: University of North Carolina Press, 1968, pp. 194–208.

Steadman, John M., *Epic and Tragic Structure in 'Paradise Lost,'* University of Chicago Press, 1976.

Steadman, John M., *Milton and the Renaissance Hero*, Oxford: Clarendon Press, 1967.
Swedenberg, Jr, H. T., *The Theory of the Epic in England: 1650–1800*, Berkeley: University of California Press, 1944.
Thomson, J. A. K., *The Classical Background of English Literature*, 1948; rpt New York: Collier, 1962.
Thomson, J. A. K., *Classical Influences on English Poetry*, London: Allen & Unwin, 1951.
Tillyard, E. M. W., *The English Epic and its Background*, London: Chatto & Windus, 1954.
Tillyard, E. M. W., 'Milton and the Classics,' *Essays by Divers Hands: Being the Transactions of the Royal Society of Literature of the United Kingdom*, XXVI (1953), 59–72.
Tillyard, E. M. W., 'Milton and the Epic,' *The Miltonic Setting*, New York: Macmillan, 1949, pp. 141–204.
Weinberg, Bernard, *A History of Literary Criticism in the Italian Renaissance*, University of Chicago Press, 2 vols, 1961.
Whaler, James, 'Animal Simile in *Paradise Lost*,' *Publications of the Modern Language Association of America*, XLVII (1932), 534–53.
Whaler, James, 'Compounding and Distribution of Similes in *Paradise Lost*,' *Modern Philology*, XXVIII (1931), 313–34.
Whaler, James, *Counterpoint and Symbol: An Inquiry into the Rhythm of Milton's Epic Simile*, Copenhagen: Rosenkilde & Bagger, 1956.
Whaler, James, 'Grammatical Nexus of the Miltonic Simile,' *Journal of English and Germanic Philology*, XXX (1931), 327–34.
Whaler, James, 'The Miltonic Simile,' *Publications of the Modern Language Association of America*, XLVI (1931), 1034–74.
White, Harold Ogden, *Plagiarism and Imitation During the English Renaissance*, Cambridge, Mass.: Harvard University Press, 1935.
Widmer, Kingsley, 'The Iconography of Renunciation: The Miltonic Simile,' *Milton's Epic Poetry*, ed. C. A. Patrides, Baltimore: Penguin, 1967, pp. 121–31.
Williams, Arnold, *The Common Expositor*, Chapel Hill: University of North Carolina Press, 1947.
Woodhouse, A. S. P., *The Heavenly Muse*, ed. Hugh MacCallum, University of Toronto Press, 1972.
Woodhull, Marianna, *The Epic of 'Paradise Lost,'* 1907; rpt New York: Gordian Press, 1968.

Index